WHAT

*When You Don't
Know What to Say
to Your Own Family*

WHAT TO DO

When You Don't Know What to Say to Your Own Family

PEGGYSUE WELLS & MARY ANN FROEHLICH

Advancing the Ministries of the Gospel
AMG *Publishers*

God's Word to you is our highest calling.

What to Do When You Don't Know What to Say to Your Own Family

Copyright © 2003 by Mary Ann Froehlich and PeggySue Wells

Published by AMG Publishers
6815 Shallowford Rd.
Chattanooga, Tennessee 37421

Unless otherwise indicated, all Scripture quotations are taken from the HOLY BIBLE, NEW INTERNATIONAL VERSION® NIV®. Copyright ©1973, 1978, 1984 by International Bible Society. Used by permission of Zondervan Publishing House. All rights reserved.

ISBN 0-89957-354-1

First printing—August 2003

Cover designed by Jennifer Ross, AMG Publishers
Interior design and typesetting by Reider Publishing Services, West Hollywood, California
Edited and Proofread by Marjorie Carlson, Dan Penwell, Warren Baker, and Sharon Neal

Printed in the United States of America
09 08 07 06 05 04 03 –D– 8 7 6 5 4 3 2 1

We dedicate this book:

To our contributors, who choose to remain anonymous.

To my husband, John,
my children, Janelle, Natalie, and Cameron,
my mom, Maria, and deceased dad, Bill,
my sister, Judy,
and my second parents, Mike and Marian.

Each has in a unique, remarkable way taught me about
the love of a family.

Mary Ann

To my children, AmyRose, Leilani, Holly, Josiah, Estee,
Hannah, and Lilyanna.

And to those friends who have been like family,
Mary Ann, June, Ilona, Christine, Dee, Saundra, and
Denise.

PeggySue

Acknowledgments

We wish to express heartfelt thanks to all our gracious contributors, who inspire and enCOURAGE us to love our families as Christ loves his church.

And to Dan Penwell and the professionals at AMG Publishers who said, "I'm in favor of anything that encourages people."

Flatter me, and I may not believe you.
Criticize me, and I may not like you.
Ignore me, and I may not forgive you.
Encourage me, and I will not forget you.

—WILLIAM ARTHUR WARD

Contents

Introduction

I n *What to Do When You Don't Know What to Say*, we explored the ministry of enCOURAGEment, giving courage to hurting people in their darkest hour. True help rarely comes in the form of advice, but from feeling someone's pain, seeing a need, and acting on that insight. True help is being "Jesus with skin on," giving hugs from God during the crises of our lives.

While interviewing contributors for the original book, we made an amazing discovery. Many people find it easier to minister to their friends, acquaintances, and even complete strangers than to their own family members. We are quicker to send a note or gift of encouragement to a close friend who is enduring a tough time than to our irritated spouse or teenager. Perhaps we minister to our friends because they appreciate our efforts and their response affirms us. In contrast, a struggling spouse, child, or parent can direct their frustration at us. Families are God's most effective instrument for teaching unconditional love and sacrifice.

Actions—tangible acts of love—speak louder than words to people experiencing crises, and no one needs our tender touch of caring *without judgment* more than the people who live in our homes or who are related to us. Our primary calling is to minister to our family members. They are our God-given top priority, our first mission field.

Nevertheless, it is all too common for the woman who delivers balanced meals to sick church members to then pick up a pizza on her way home for her own family. Likewise the administrator of an outreach program for seniors lacks time to drive his own aging mother to the market or to medical appointments. Imagine the graduate student who is so immersed in completing his doctorate in family counseling that he is unable to spend time with his own teenagers.

Our culture reinforces this kind of behavior. When family time is already scarce and the family dinner hour is becoming extinct, communities and schools schedule committee meetings and parenting seminars on weeknights. To attend sessions on topics such as "Helping Your Kids with Homework," "Improving Communication with Your Teens," or "Building Self-Esteem," parents must leave their children home alone or with a baby-sitter. Parenting seminars are helpful, but let's think outside the box. Workshops on communicating with teens could be offered on Saturday mornings when most teens are sound asleep.

We are not advocating ingrown families that only minister to their own. Service programs and ministries in the community are important, but they should be an outgrowth of caring for our families—an overflow, not a substitute. We have to make a conscious effort to avoid giving our families the leftovers, to avoid denying them our firstfruits.

In this sequel, *What to Do When You Don't Know What to Say to Your Own Family,* we honor those who minister in unique ways to their spouses, children, parents, siblings, and extended family members in the different seasons of life.

Most stories in this book are about people helping family members in crisis. Many contributors shared ideas for preventing crisis and nurturing families so we are prepared to cope when a crisis comes. We included a few "unhelps," actions that are not helpful to family members in crisis.

Contributors to this sequel have provided a variety of illustrations. One offers suggestions for ministering to a six-year-old, while another shares quite different ideas for encouraging a young adult who has left the nest. Young married couples inspire us with fresh ideas, while the "marathoners," those married twenty-five years or longer, strengthen our long-haul commitment with their wisdom. Our circle of ministry expands when we serve as the hands of Jesus to siblings, aunts and uncles, cousins, grandparents, and in-laws.

This book is about *family*. The final section expands the definition to include our church family and our friends, who are our "adopted" family. They too need to be encouraged when they are experiencing conflicts or grieving the loss of loved ones.

We invite you to creatively explore the ministry to which God has called you. On a bad day, you may sometimes view your family as a time-consuming obstacle to your "important" outside ministries or professional pursuits, but your loved ones are your central life mission. You are the hands of Jesus to your family. Celebrate your invisible, most powerful ministry.

The Habit Prescription

An ounce of prevention is worth a pound of cure.

Prevention is the best medicine and less expensive than treatment of a diagnosed physical disease. Daily exercise and staying on a low-fat diet may be inconvenient today, but not as traumatic as bypass surgery or chemotherapy tomorrow.

The same is true in family life. With a little daily effort we can avoid major blockages or growing tumors that are often not discovered until it is too late. With preventive measures and early detection, we can uncover family problems in the beginning stages before an unsurvivable crisis descends.

Resiliency experts have studied the positive traits of children and adults who successfully survive crises and challenging life circumstances. We agree with these experts when they say that too much focus has been placed on what families are doing wrong. We wrote this book to show what families are doing *right*. These pages are filled with stories contributed by normal people living ordinary lives with *extraordinary* relationships.

In the original *What to Do When You Don't Know What to Say*, we discovered that most people reach out with acts of TLC (tender loving care) to friends more easily than to their own family members. In this sequel we made a second, amazing, and more important discovery. A handful of thoughtful acts sprinkled throughout the year doesn't make a dent. You can't fill an emotional gas tank with a dropper. Family members with loving, healthy relationships nurture one another with caring acts on a regular basis. They develop a consistent pattern, a habit that can be counted on through the ups and downs of life.

These habits can be informal rituals or longstanding traditions. Such habits are "relationship glue," cementing family bonds and occasionally preventing a crisis entirely. Other times these practices help a family survive a crisis with established opportunities for staying connected, communicating, and working through problems. The time to start brainstorming about rituals or thoughtful deeds is not *during* a crisis. That's too late. Good habits must already be in place.

For example, for years Mary Ann's girlfriend served pumpkin soup on Halloween evening. Her son grew up and left home to pursue a rebellious and destructive lifestyle. His parents did not see him for months. They did not know if he was dead or alive until they answered a knock at the door on Halloween night, and there stood their son. "I've come to eat pumpkin soup with my family," he said. He returned on Christmas Eve to share their traditional clam chowder. What seemed like frivolous traditions were lifelines in the crisis, opportunities for this prodigal to reconnect.

In the course of our research we asked numerous families, "How did you nurture your spouse, child, parent, or relative through life's major crises?" Most families who responded focused on their relationship rituals.

Yet there are few guarantees in life. Mary Ann's beloved father walked miles every day and ate an exemplary diet. He didn't smoke or drink. He loved life and did everything he could to be healthy. Ironically he died within hours of bypass heart surgery. We both know marriages and families who, in spite of all the effort they have invested, do not make it out of intensive care. We honor them in our book, too.

We have purposely not included a separate chapter on stepfamilies. As children we both were part of blended families and know that differentiating family members only causes pain. Separating blood relatives from "adopted" ones can damage fragile relationships. Our hope is that you will apply the ideas of our contributors to all types of family relationships.

> *To get the full value of a joy you must have someone to divide it with.*
>
> MARK TWAIN

No Shortcuts

You can spell love a thousand different ways.

VIRGINIA REYNOLDS

Unlike PeggySue who raises horses, Mary Ann is not very good with animals. Yet her children have convinced her that dogs, fish, mice, hamsters, and rabbits are necessary to a happy childhood.

Their latest addition is a rescue dog, a strong-willed basset hound named Barney. Their previous dog, a large Labrador, used to knock Mary Ann over. She was under the mistaken impression that basset hounds were too close to the ground to push over their owners. To her surprise, Barney's long and low physique translated into long and tall when he stood on his hind legs. Mary Ann was also naïve about stubbornness being a common trait in hounds. When ninety-pound Barney wanted to push Mary Ann over, he did.

It didn't take long to discover why Barney was a rescue dog. His original family couldn't handle him and couldn't wait to get rid of him. Within a week of arriving at Mary Ann's home, Barney was stealing food off the kitchen counter, urinating throughout the house, and chewing everything in sight. One day she found him standing on the new couch, eating all the pillows. During the holidays he stole and consumed an entire box of dark chocolate truffles and had to be rushed to the veterinary emergency room to have his stomach pumped. Barney was an accident waiting to happen.

Barney was enrolled in obedience training, a kind of basset boot camp. If you have a dog, you already know that the instructor primarily trained the owners. The trainer taught them many tricks for handling the dog, but he emphasized, "Your dog will never obey you if you do not take the time to develop a relationship with him. You will have no influence if he does not respect you." That was the most important message.

It is common sense. We can never influence those with whom we have no relationship. Relationships require an investment of time, and there are no short-cuts. There are no shortcuts with stubborn basset hounds, with spouses, with children, with parents, with our church family, *or with God.*

The theme that emerges from what our contributors have shared is that nurturing families requires *time*. Every story in this book represents an investment of time, a precious commodity in our fast-paced culture. We must purposely take the time to love and connect with our families in creative and unique ways.

Stories from our contributors have been divided into four sections: Marriage, Children, Other Relatives, and Expanded Family. Each section begins with our own introductory comments and then presents our contributors' ideas for **what to do when you don't know what to say to your own family.**

Family faces are magic mirrors.
Looking at people who belong to us,
we see the past, present, and future.

GAIL LUMET BUCKLEY

SECTION I

Marriage

In the name of God,
I take you to be my wife/husband,
To have and to hold from this day forward,
For better for worse,
For richer for poorer,
In sickness and in health,
To love and to cherish,
Until death do us part.
This is my solemn vow.

Did you make this solemn vow five years ago? Twenty years ago? Fifty years ago? You probably already know the sharp contrast between the sacred promise you made on your wedding day and the daily realities of marriage in the obstacle course of life. "For better for *worse*, for richer for *poorer*, in *sickness* and in health"—as you repeated those words, you never imagined the endurance test that lay before you. You would not have believed anyone who tried to explain that making a marriage work is a rigorous task, a challenge impossible to understand until experienced. This lifelong commitment is the truest and most difficult test of our faith.

A Barna research survey indicates that Christians have a higher divorce rate than non-Christians and evangelical Christians have the highest divorce rate of all groups.

Perseverance only counts when we most want to give up. A vow—a promise, a binding oath—has its greatest value when we are most tempted to break it. An oath would be unnecessary if marriage were an easy path. Contrary to what many in our culture believe, there is no return policy on a marriage. Not *if* hard times come, but *when* hard times come, will we remain faithful to God and our vow?

Author Lewis Smedes said, "There are two kinds of writers: smart ones and dumb ones. The smart kind write what they know. The dumb kind write in order to know." We wanted to know what couples with enduring marriages did to nurture their relationships. How did these partnerships not just survive, but thrive? When we researched the subject, one theme emerged.

These couples did not simply "let their marriage happen." On the contrary, they knew the desired end result (until death do us part) and purposely made an extra effort to care for their spouses.

Chapter three cites examples from all seasons of marriage, while chapter four offers the advice of marriage "experts"—not counselors, but marathoners who have been married twenty-five years or longer.

In a letter to advice columnist Ann Landers, a wife wrote that a serious car accident had changed her husband from a happy and fun-loving person to a hostile and inattentive man. He could not keep a full-time job, had no interest in sex, and belittled his wife. Ann Landers replied:

Dear Despaired Wife:

I suspect your husband's car accident may have caused some serious brain damage that affected his personality. Find out from his doctor if anything can be done about it. If your husband refuses to get the help he needs, I say dump him.

What to Do When You Don't Know What to Say to . . . Your Spouse *(during the early years of marriage)*

Two are better than one,
because they have a good return for their work:
If one falls down,
his friend can help him up.
But pity the man who falls
and has no one to help him up!
Also, if two lie down together, they will keep warm.
But how can one keep warm alone?

ECCLESIASTES 4:9–11

My husband calls every morning from his office to check on me and ask how he can help. He offers to run errands during his lunch hour or pick up groceries on the way home. With an infant and a preschooler at home, I appreciate his thoughtfulness. When our family has experienced illness or other emergencies, his willingness to help carry the load has been my lifeline.

Whenever I traveled on business, my wife hid presents in my suitcase such as cards, pictures drawn by our kids, candy bars, magazines, and paperback books. Sometimes the presents were labeled, "Open on day number one," "Open on day number two," and so on for the length of my trip. This practice kept my family close to me when I struggled with loneliness and temptation.

As part of his job, my husband often attends meetings in exclusive hotels with premiere maid service. He is served meals created by world-class chefs while I am cleaning up messes and eating macaroni and cheese with our young children at home. Sometimes when I have had a bad day (if he is in town), my husband will turn down my side of the bed and leave a rose with two mints on my pillow.

Every guest at our wedding was asked to write us a letter to be opened on a particular anniversary. Each year we open one of those letters filled with anniversary greetings and advice about marriage from a special person who was present when we took our marriage vows. In an instant we are transported back to that memorable day when our lives and hearts were joined together.

When I was diagnosed with breast cancer, I spent two years in chemotherapy. To take care of our children, our home, and me, my husband curtailed his travel schedule and began working from a home office. Immersed in my own battle with cancer, I did not realize how difficult and stressful this ordeal was for my husband. I was the last person who could help him. His friend living in another state, whose wife had survived breast cancer, began calling my husband to offer moral support and lend a listening ear. Because of his friend's support, my husband was better equipped to encourage me. Now every week my husband calls another friend whose wife was recently diagnosed with ovarian cancer.

During our first year of marriage my husband traveled with other salespeople for a major company. They were together all week, and then on Friday nights they gathered at a local bar for a drink after returning from the airport. Instead of participating in this Friday ritual, my husband came directly home. He told me, "I've been with salespeople all week. The person I can't wait to see is you." It is not surprising that many of his coworkers' marriages were in trouble.

Working for InterVarsity during the first fifteen years of our marriage brought challenges to our relationship. With little free time, less money, and three children, the typical date night was unrealistic. College kids were at our home every night for student meetings and Bible studies. One couple encouraged us to carve out time for each other and offered to baby-sit for our children once a week. We spent this free time nurturing our relationship by going out for coffee, taking walks, or having picnics. At that point we were making time for each other, but we still didn't have spending money. One day I returned from a "prayer walk" to find mail from missionary friends in China. They certainly had no more money than we did, but they had enclosed a check for one hundred dollars in the envelope. "For the love of Christ," read the attached message. We cashed that check and set the money aside to be used for our couple outings. It was wise to invest in our marriage.

My husband got more than he bargained for when he married me. Of the three children he inherited from my first marriage, one was an angry teenage boy and another was a daughter with diabetes. Then I became critically ill—someday I may need a kidney transplant. My husband has sought the advice of other men about parenting the children, has settled our family in a church, and has helped cook meals and wash clothes. The situation has stretched him, and he has responded in love.

Sometimes wives feel as if they are invisible; they feel that their efforts are unappreciated. Realizing this, my husband sent me a "lifetime thank-you note" on our twentieth anniversary. He specifically thanked me for all the things I thought he took for granted such as doing the laundry, changing the sheets, going to the market, and taking out the trash. He listed mundane tasks that I thought he never noticed. He thanked me for taking loving care of him for two decades.

When I am experiencing a difficult time at work, my wife sends cards to me at the office. Sometimes she includes funny cartoons. The message remains, "I believe in you. Hang in there! I love you. Thanks for working hard to take care of our family." Her thoughtfulness brightens my entire day.

In premarital counseling we decided that we would reconnect within twenty minutes of any disagreement. We felt that "not letting the sun go down on our anger" was not soon enough for us. We didn't want to start any bad habits such as the silent treatment. Nor did we want unresolved issues to take root. Whether we agree or not, we start working on our relationship again within twenty minutes.

When I fell and broke my neck, the doctors told me that I would be paralyzed for the rest of my life. My husband loved me too much to accept their diagnosis. He located the best specialists and arranged for me to be airlifted to another state to meet with them. With his support I went through the treatments the specialists recommended, and today I walk with a cane. My husband did for me what I could not do for myself. He gave me love, hope, and the ability to walk beside him.

I regularly bring flowers to my wife. Each evening I read to the children and put them to bed so that my wife can have an hour all to herself. Once a week I cook dinner and care for the children so she can have the night off to attend a Bible study, go shopping, soak in the tub, read a book, or go to bed early. The rewards of being married to a happy, valued, rested wife are more than worth the effort. And I am closer to my children than most dads I know because I spend time with them every day. My brother-in-law told me he gets in trouble each time I bring my wife flowers. I told him he ought to try it.

We were married on July 18 nearly two decades ago. On the eighteenth of every month, my husband leaves a surprise for me. I may find the gift in the house, in the garage, on the seat of my car, or in the yard. The gift may be a Post-it love note or poem, a single rose, a chocolate truffle, a coupon for coffee, or a handwritten invitation to dinner. Sometimes he sends a card to me at work. His creativity is endless and though I have come to expect my treat on the eighteenth of each month, I am always surprised at what he has planned.

Spouses can be dream cheerleaders or dream squashers. I dreamed of becoming a freelance writer. My wife not only encouraged my dream, but also typed my manuscripts and worked to supplement our income through the lean years. Today I support my family as a professional writer because my wife believed in my dream and came alongside to make it a reality.

As a teenager I was sexually abused at home, a secret I kept even after I was married. As God began his healing process in my life, I shared my background with my husband. His unconditional love and acceptance of me in spite of the ugliness of my past has been the perfect example of God's love and mercy. My husband and the arms he wraps around me have been instrumental in freeing me from my pain and shame.

When I return exhausted from a long business trip, my wife throws me a party, complete with banners, streamers, and refreshments. She and our kids jump out from behind the couch and shout, "Surprise!" and "Welcome home!" Friends have told me that when they return, their wives give them the cold shoulder, a form of payback for the lonely week. Business trips are not glamorous or fun. Though she is tired too, my wife makes an effort to lift my spirits and paves the way for a restful weekend.

As the daughter of an air force officer, I thought being punctual meant being early to an event. My husband marched to a different clock and was consistently late. This difference was a constant source of irritation, especially on Sunday mornings as we prepared to go to church. No matter how we addressed the problem, it grew worse. One Sunday while my sons and I were waiting in the car for my husband, I said, "You know what, boys? If I got fifty cents every time Dad was late, I could buy a candy bar." Then the solution hit me! We decided to pit our weaknesses against each other. Every time he was late, I would indulge in a candy bar. Every time I ate a candy bar, he was allowed to be late. After fifteen years of conflict over this issue, my husband's tardiness immediately stopped, and my candy addiction faded into history. Instead of being critical, we were committed to each other's success and well-being.

My wife was in her late twenties when we married. Waiting for the man she would marry, she had remained pure. Her lifetime faithfulness is the most beautiful gift she could have given to me. Wanting to symbolize her gift, she arranged for the purity ring she had worn for over a decade to be melted into my wedding band.

Whenever my husband returns from a trip, he takes our family out to dinner at one of our favorite restaurants. Eating at another restaurant is the last thing that he wants to do after a week of travel, but my husband realizes that we need some pampering and a break from our routine at home. He gained this insight from a mentor/boss who, having been divorced, advised my husband that an ounce of prevention is worth a pound of cure.

Through a number of poor choices and economic downturns, my husband and I found ourselves in debt. My husband took a second job that required him to work in the evenings and on weekends. His second job was menial, but it paid the bills and his extra effort assured me that he would provide for our family even in hard times. My husband assumed full responsibility and did what was needed to take care of us. His provision gave the children and me a sense of security.

I am a better pastor and marriage counselor today because I did not get straight A's in my seminary classes. Like any other professional graduate program, seminary training is physically and intellectually taxing. In the early years of our marriage I would stay up late to attack mountains of work after my wife went to bed. My studies and our part-time jobs prevented us from spending much time together. My brother's marriage had not survived law school, and a friend had nearly divorced after attending medical school. I didn't want that to happen to us. Then a wise professor said in class, "Now don't you dare tell your wife that you cannot come to bed tonight because you have to write a paper on the Song of Solomon!" I realized the irony in my life: studying *about* God was becoming more important than living *for* God. I did not receive the highest grades in my classes, but my marriage remained intact through that stressful period.

Years ago I was diagnosed with lupus. When my husband learned that playing the piano can help relieve hand pain, he surprised me by having a baby grand piano delivered to our home. It is a player piano, so I can enjoy the music even when I am not practicing. Though I am still in the elementary stages of learning to play the piano, my husband is proud of me. He enthusiastically encourages my progress.

My wife and I both work hard and lead stressful lives. Our hectic schedules cause many conflicts over the family calendar. To alleviate some of the stress, we have mutually set apart some "pampering days" for each other. On my wife's pampering days we either go out for dinner to an elegant restaurant or I serve her breakfast in bed. My pampering days are New Year's Day and Super Bowl Sunday. I lie on the couch and watch football while she serves my favorite appetizers and chili. These are the best days of the entire year.

When I was promoted to a high management position, my wife asked other leaders to write letters of advice and support to me. She collected those letters and gave them to me just before I assumed my new title. Her thoughtfulness provided me with the encouragement and words of wisdom I needed. I appreciate those letters and know I can contact these leaders for advice anytime.

Our married friends were always talking about their weekly date nights. We liked the idea, but with three children and a limited income, my husband and I could not afford to pay a baby-sitter and go out to dinner. We opted to have date nights at home. Once a week, the kids ate dinner early, got ready for bed, and watched a movie upstairs. I set the table with scented candles, linens, and crystal, and put soft jazz on the stereo. Sometimes I cooked dinner, and other times my husband cooked or brought home takeout food. The date continued as we washed dishes together. We didn't need to leave the house or spend money to reconnect at the end of the week.

My job requires frequent travel, which involves flying around the country and spending lonely nights in hotels. My wife makes a point of knowing my favorite authors and buying me books to take on my trips. When I am enjoying a series, she purchases the sequel just as I am finishing the previous book. Sometimes she puts a note or a candy bar in the new book. These book companions tell me that my wife is thinking of me.

I tend to become involved in too many activities, especially church programs. Instead of complaining about my busy schedule, my husband plans a special event for us from going out for dinner and a movie to a weekend getaway trip. Of course I never turn down his invitations. His creativity tells me that I am valuable to him and a priority in his life.

As a counselor I spend all day listening to other people's problems. The last thing I want to do when I come home at night is to listen. But my wife, a true verbal processor with a stressful job of her own, needs to unload *everything* each evening. How can I deny her the one skill I practice all day? Do I only care and listen when I am being paid for my time? The most loving response to her need is to listen with the same compassion and attention that I offer my patients.

Throughout the years my husband and I have kept a journal, recording what we did on our anniversaries, birthdays, and other memorable days. When celebrating our anniversary, we enjoy reading about our previous anniversary dates. When celebrating birthdays, we relive past birthday memories. We also keep a section for brainstorming about goals and dreams. In our old age it will be fun to see which ones were fulfilled.

I work long hours in a stressful job and am exhausted at the end of the day. It may seem old-fashioned and politically incorrect, but I am grateful that my wife supports me by having dinner ready when I come home. No matter how late, we have a nightly family dinner with our children and discussion of conflicts is banned while we are eating. After dinner I relax while watching a ball game, and my wife washes the dishes. I couldn't face the next day's pressures without this haven of rest that she provides. After caring for our children and working in her part-time business, my wife is tired too, yet she sacrificially ministers to me.

Before my husband jets out of town on a business trip, he carves out time to make sure the bills are paid, the car is in good working order, and the house maintenance is up-to-date. His efforts tangibly tell me how much he loves me. He knows that when he is away, I must assume his responsibilities around the home. His thoughtfulness makes my week easier.

As a guest professor at several college campuses, I sometimes need to be in two places at the same time. As one class is ending, another is beginning. My wife saves the day by administering the final exam in one class while I begin teaching another. She also attends my musical performances and hosts my annual office Christmas party. Our partnership continues as I help her make and market her crafts at festivals. And we are committed to spending one to two annual vacation weeks away from our hectic schedules.

My husband and I celebrate our anniversary every month. We compete to be the first one who remembers the date. Because I am a fanatical list keeper with a busy schedule, one month he gave me personalized checklists he had created on the computer. These thoughtful gestures say that he understands and accepts me the way I am. Though he has his own demanding career, he doesn't mind going out for dinner when I am too tired to cook after teaching all day. My husband helps me take my students on field trips and camping excursions. He often types my paperwork and does household chores. Daily he communicates the fact that he is genuinely committed to supporting my success.

Once a week the children and I meet my husband at his office, and we have lunch together. Sometimes I pack a picnic, other times we eat at a restaurant. Before and after lunch there are opportunities to get to know the people my husband works with and catch a glimpse of his workaday world. The children bring pictures they have colored to post in their daddy's workstation, and they feel loved when they see their photos on his desk. By meeting at my husband's office each week, our family has bridged the worlds of home and work.

Woman was taken out of man;
not out of his head to top him,
nor out of his feet to be trampled underfoot;
but out of his side to be equal to him,
under his arm to be protected,
and near his heart to be loved.

MATTHEW HENRY

What to Do When You Don't Know What to Say to . . . Your Spouse *(even after many years of marriage)*

Marriage with the long view comes with the conviction that nothing will break us up . . . this kind of commitment is not made just once, but over and over through the course of a lifetime. We cling to it during the dark nights of the soul that come to nearly every marriage, times when the love is hard to feel but the promise keeps us together.

WILLIAM DOHERTY

My wife and I have been married for forty years. I attribute our success to one simple habit. At the end of every day I ask my wife to review her day for me, and she listens as I do the same. I want her to know that I value what she does with her life. Even when we are apart, we conduct our daily life review by telephone. This practice has kept us close during the tough times of life. The most important gift that I can give another human being, especially my wife, is my precious *time*. I do not wait for a crisis to support her; I offer support every day.

The key to our lasting marriage has been simple and inexpensive. Every night after dinner we walk the dog. As newlyweds we had to walk the dog every night because we lived in a confining apartment. When we had babies, I enjoyed getting out of the house, pushing our baby in a stroller, and listening to my husband talk about his day. When we had older children and teens, walking the dog provided needed time alone to discuss issues involving our kids. Now that we are in the empty-nest stage of life, we walk the dog because we need the exercise. The dogs have changed over the years, but walking the dog is a lifelong habit which, I am sure, has saved us thousands of dollars in therapy.

My husband and I have been married for forty-five years. We celebrate all of our anniversaries, but every five years my husband surprises me with an extra special overnight trip. On our twenty-fifth anniversary he took me to New York to see a show. On our fortieth anniversary a limo arrived at our home and took me to the coastline where my husband was waiting for me at a bed-and-breakfast inn. Anniversaries are the birthdays of our marriage.

Early in our marriage we established three habits that have sustained us through thirty-two years of life's challenges. First, we agreed to fight fair. No matter how tempting it was to bring up past incidents, we only dealt with the issue at hand. Second, we agreed never to complain about one another to our children or parents. Problems with each other needed to be discussed and resolved between the two of us. Third, and most important, we stayed close by praying aloud together every night before bed. While praying, we learn about each other's individual struggles, and we are united as we bring our shared concerns to God.

In the beginning I didn't respect my husband. We struggled as I made it clear that my career came first. My husband was gentle and supportive, which I interpreted as a sign of weakness. He wanted children, but I was unwilling to interrupt my fast-track promotions for motherhood. Then I suddenly became ill, suffering from a host of physical problems including chronic fatigue syndrome. Overnight my life changed. I could no longer bring home a big paycheck or enjoy stimulating business lunches. I couldn't get out of bed, let alone fix my hair or put on makeup. I was physically unattractive and, because of my bitterness and frustration, equally unattractive inside. My husband never complained. He lovingly cared for me, even as I raged at him. It was then that I began to understand that his kind gentleness was not weakness, but a tremendous strength that I did not possess. In sickness or in health, in drivenness or in bitterness, my husband remained faithful to our wedding vows. His patient love melted my heart and today he is my hero.

A lasting marriage requires creativity and improvising within one's limitations. My husband and I have always lived with financial pressures. We have known seasons of famine when he was unemployed. As a result, our love life was strained. Books about marriage suggested romantic ways to recharge our love life. Friends counseled us to have a date night or to get away for the weekend. But baby-sitters, restaurants, and hotels all cost money. We felt trapped. We had to improvise. On our fifteenth wedding anniversary I sent our kids to my parents' house, lit a fire in the fireplace, made a nice dinner, and we ate by candlelight. I wanted to buy sexy new lingerie to surprise my husband, but I couldn't afford such luxuries. One of my husband's favorite nightgowns was an old flannel thing I'd worn forever. He loved the soft fabric, but I hated the "granny gown" feeling I had when I wore it. In honor of our anniversary, I sewed the gown into a sexy teddy. Igniting romance takes a little effort, but not necessarily a lot of money.

Every year on my birthday my wife and our children present me with a book containing heartfelt expressions and pictures representing the past twelve months. The book was short and simple when the children were young, but twenty-five years later the book has become a chronicle of our family's life. I look forward to receiving my special annual gift, and I look through these books whenever I need to take solace in the comfort of family.

A supportive spouse is a dream catcher. Being an entre-preneur who enjoys starting new businesses, I have taken several risks during our married life. Each time my wife has encouraged my dreams and affirmed that she trusts me and believes in me. She has been willing to work in her home business to cover extra expenses. With her words and actions she cheers, "Go for your dreams." This is the same message we give our children as they explore opportunities.

My parents, who are now deceased, were married for sixty years. The one marriage lesson they modeled for me was true companionship. They took turns reading to each other. While my mom folded laundry, my dad read to her. While one washed dishes, the other read. While one drove the car on a long trip, the other read aloud. They would have found today's books on tape pointless. They read to one another to keep each other company during life's bor-ing tasks. Mom and Dad also enjoyed discussing what they read. Often they included us, their children, in the rotating reading habit. We would read to them as they did chores, and they would do the same for us. With that immersion in the world of literature, we obviously all learned to love books. More important than the educational benefits of our upbringing was what we learned about how marriage partners share daily life and support one another. Reading is only one type of marriage glue. While my sister-in-law washes dinner dishes, my brother dries them as he sings her favorite Broadway show tunes. My brother is not a good singer, which makes his efforts more entertaining. But they are together, giving each other the foundation of companionship, the gift of presence.

Married over thirty years, my wife and I informally renew our vows every anniversary. Usually the ceremony remains private with just the two of us present, though we included our children and close friends on our twenty-fifth anniversary. Each year we rewrite the traditional vows, depending on recent challenges in our lives. For example, we focused on "in sickness and health" when my wife was recovering from breast cancer. "For richer or poorer" was the theme when I had been unemployed for several months. We highlighted "for better or worse" when one of our teenagers was struggling with drug addiction. We never want to forget that we made a promise to stand by each other no matter what the future holds.

As I was flying home from a stressful business trip twenty years ago, the older man seated next to me asked, "Son, what are you going to do when you get home?" We had already discussed our common sales profession, and he knew that I had a family. I replied, "I am tired. I am going to crash on the couch and watch weekend sports." Then came the words of wisdom that I have never forgotten, "I wouldn't advise that. Your wife is your best client. She's probably had a hard week with the kids. Bring your wife flowers. Wine and dine her because she is your most important account." I took those words to heart, and my wife and I have been happily married for thirty years.

In our early years of marriage my wife and I could not afford expensive restaurant dinners, so we met for breakfast once a week. Since we both were attending school and working evening jobs, we had crazy schedules. We decided to put any issues that were troubling us on the shelf during our weekly breakfast and focus on our relationship. We asked good questions, as we did when we were dating, to catch up on each other's lives. Later, when we had more money and time, we traded breakfast for Friday night dinner at romantic restaurants with candlelit tables and soft music. But we were both tired and ended up discussing the latest crisis with our children or arguing about the week's problems. One day we realized that we were happier when we were struggling newlyweds. Thirty years later we have reinstated our breakfasts on Tuesday mornings when we are fresh and awake and the problems of the week have not accumulated. When our teenage son backs our new car into a pole, or my aging mother needs to be hospitalized, or our daughter at college runs out of money, or the refrigerator breaks down, we are better prepared to face those challenges because our lines of communication are open.

Occasionally people ask me if I am resentful toward my wife. My answer is no because one's attitude is a choice. No one entering marriage truly knows what that relationship will hold for a lifetime. Sometimes the traits that attract us to our mate are a double-edged sword. I married a dynamic, exciting, successful career woman and later discovered that she was also a workaholic who never intended to take time out to have a family. Marriage is not a contract, not a mutually beneficial agreement to exchange services. Biblical marriage is a covenant, a promise we keep regardless of our mate's response. "Husbands, love your wives, just as Christ loved the church" (Ephesians 5:25).

Reliving memories is important to a lasting relationship. Our first date was twenty-six years ago at a hamburger joint at the pier. The date was May 10. Obviously we hit it off, and we have eaten hamburgers and fries at that restaurant on May 10 ever since. We have lived in different parts of the state, but every year we travel back for the anniversary of our first date.

My husband had a grueling travel schedule in the early years of our marriage. I did my best to be strong, manage the household, and be both mother and father to our children. As our school-age children grew older and life's demands increased, I felt like a failure because I couldn't keep the pace anymore. Finally, I told my husband I was overwhelmed. He graciously responded, "Why didn't you tell me sooner?" He immediately changed jobs, and we relocated to a situation where we could raise our family together. Today we enjoy time with our grown children and our grandchildren in between the business trips we take together.

As newlyweds my husband and I decided that no matter how angry we were, there were three things we would never do: sleep in separate rooms, threaten divorce, or say that we hated each other. Of course we have been most tempted to break this agreement when we most desperately needed to keep it. Sometimes we have almost bitten our tongues off! Sometimes I have slept on the far edge of our bed. But we have stayed married for thirty-five years, and we have encouraged our newlywed adult children to set ground rules in their marriages as early as possible.

My young adult daughter recently asked, "How did you and Dad develop such a great marriage?" My husband and I laughed, thinking, *Did she grow up in the same house that we live in?* We certainly had our share of conflicts and tough times. Then I realized that she didn't say a "happy" marriage; she said a "great" marriage. A great marriage is not a perfect marriage; by definition, marriage *cannot* be problem-free. A great marriage is two people who endure conflict yet stay together, morning after morning, night after night, because they made a promise.

My dad labored at a factory to support our family. My mom arranged her schedule around his. When he worked the 5:00 A.M. shift, she served him a hearty breakfast at 4:00 A.M. When he worked the night shift, she served him a full course dinner at 3:00 P.M. No matter how inconvenient, she physically and emotionally nurtured my dad. She would find today's family complaints about not being able to connect or have a meal together strange. She always said, "Where there is a will, there is a way."

After sixty years of marriage, my wife died just days before Christmas. Although we agreed that our ashes would be scattered over the mountains, I could not bear to part with hers. Throughout our marriage my wife would say, "You don't know how much I love you," and I would reply, "Likewise." I could never say, "I love you." I would write poetry to her, but I couldn't say those three words. When my wife lay dying and I thought that she was comatose, I told her, "There aren't enough words to tell you how much I love you." She whispered, "Not enough words," and died. Now her ashes are on my dresser where I tell her several times a day how much I love her. But it's too late.

Success in marriage is much more than finding the right person;
it is a matter of being the right person.

Marriage partners should be soul mates, not cell mates.

Children

*Train a child in the way he should go,
and when he is old he will not turn
from it.*

PROVERBS 22:6

We are stewards in each of our family relationships, yet we sense that role most intensely as we care for the children God gave us. This section focuses on nurturing our children at various stages of life. One chapter is devoted to younger children, followed by two chapters that explore the unique challenge of caring for teenagers. The final chapter addresses our adult children and the cords of relationship that become more elastic whether they are away at college for the first time or leading separate adult lives.

As you read these entries, you may not agree with some of the approaches taken by our contributors. Here lies the key to family life. What works for one child or family does not necessarily work for another. Our individual families are not apples and oranges—they are watermelons and kiwis! The most courageous parents we know are those who do what is best for their child no matter what anybody else thinks. Outward impressions are meaningless. God looks at our hearts, and our family members do the same.

A wise counselor pointed out that Proverbs 22:6 is often misinterpreted. The verse does not mean that there is one correct set of standards for training children and that parents who adhere to those standards are guaranteed to have godly children. "Train a child in the way he should go" refers to understanding the individuality and natural bent of a child and encouraging his growth and spirituality from that perspective. Our job is to tailor our acts of nurturing to each child.

Neither of us grew up in the church or in a Christian home. However, Mary Ann was raised in a remarkably loving, wise, moral, stable home and was afforded every imaginable opportunity. She can see now that God had his hand on her life and her parents' lives decades before they recognized it. In contrast, PeggySue suffered abuse and neglect in her parents' home. Our childhoods could not have been more different. Yet we have both asked exactly the same questions: How do we raise children who feel loved by God and us? How do we raise children with authentic faith?

Many Christians who were not raised in Christian homes have a vibrant, dynamic faith today. We can relate to their conversion experiences when God broke into their lives in miraculous ways. Conversely, many teens and adults who were reared in loving Christian homes have turned away from God. No parent consciously sets out to alienate their children or discourage them from following God, yet many youngsters struggle with their faith.

Ted Bundy, the serial killer, was raised in a Christian home. Marilyn Manson, ordained in the First Church of Satan, attended a Christian school. Accusing Christianity of making people weak, he now states that his band's role is to awaken a collective disbelief in Christianity. Manson was raised in a home with the trappings of Christianity, but not the love and grace of Christ. His parents made sure that he was in church every Sunday morning, but his dad rarely had time for him, except when disciplining Manson with a belt.

A friend of ours was raised by a manic-depressive mother in an abusive home. The abuse was their guarded family secret. Though her parents were active in numerous church activities, our friend shared that it would have been better for her faith if she had been raised in a non-Christian home than in a home where Christianity coexisted with abuse. She spent years in therapy untangling that confusion.

Our role as parents, especially Christian parents, is terrifyingly powerful.

> *Train up a child in the way he should go—and walk there yourself once in a while.*

JOSH BILLINGS

What to Do When You Don't Know What to Say to . . . Your Young Children

> *Children need more than food, shelter, and clothing. They need at least one person who is crazy about them.*
>
> FRAN STOTT

When I was growing up, my parents kept an "SOS" emergency can in the kitchen. They filled the can with coupons for local eateries like the ice cream store, coffee shop, and bakery. Whenever I was having a bad day or couldn't get along with anyone, I was sent to the SOS can instead of being sent to my room. I would pull out a coupon and after dinner one of my parents and I would go out for a treat. Many families would view this practice as rewarding bad moods, but my parents understood that I needed to talk one-on-one about what was bothering me. Whether I was angry with my parents or had endured a humiliating experience at school, I poured out my problems as Mom or Dad listened. When my siblings and I became teenagers, we would sometimes grab an SOS coupon and go with each other to work out a conflict. Occasionally even Mom and Dad used those SOS coupons when they needed to have serious talks. When we returned from SOS time, we felt calm and connected. This habit has followed me into adulthood. Whenever I am having a problem with a coworker, my spouse, or a friend, I find myself saying, "Let's go get ice cream and talk about this." It's hard to stay mad at someone over a hot fudge sundae.

My parents never gave us children an allowance. They believed that household chores were part of our responsibility to the family. Knowing that we also needed extra money, they kept a box of mind-challenging puzzles handy and we received payment for solving them. This encouraged us as adults to become creative problem solvers and successfully face life's challenges and obstacles.

After my divorce I wanted my children to know that there were still people who could be trusted, that there were good people who could be a positive part of their lives. I deliberately sought out opportunities for each child to play on sports teams with encouraging coaches, to go on short-term mission trips with godly missionaries, and to go on lunch dates with their pastor, school principal, and teacher. It took effort on my part, but these people were receptive to my idea and with their help my children developed a healthy view of relationships.

Mama kept an open Bible in the kitchen where she could refer to it throughout the day as thoughts and conversations led her. Her example taught me that the Bible is a part of daily life, not a book only read at church on Sundays. During family devotions Mama encouraged us to underline favorite verses, memorize them, and integrate God's Word into the fabric of our lives. Whenever we had an important decision to make, she wanted us to know what God said about it, independent of human opinion.

Ever since I was a toddler, my parents have celebrated my birth date every month of the year. I was born on May 23, so the twenty-third of each month was my special day. Breakfast included a candle on my plate, a special song, and a small gift. Sometimes my parents planned a fun outing. My half-birthday was another big event, one that could include friends. Now that I am away at college, my parents still remember my monthly special day with a phone call, card, or care package. Sometimes these surprises arrive when I am in the midst of midterms, relational problems, or other pressures. This tradition is a big hug sent through the mail.

As children we called it "trust time." Mom originally named it "truce time," but we didn't understand that term, so we changed it. Every night Mom would pray with us, tell funny stories with characters named after us, and end with truce/trust time when we could pour out any frustrations about the day. Mom promised not to judge us or instruct us, even when our complaints were about her. She simply listened. She told us that every morning brings a brand new day and encouraged us to unload our "junk" at night so we could start afresh the next day. Today as an adult I unload my "junk" to

God before I fall asleep. I clean out all resentments, grudges, or unforgivingness before the new day starts. I know that the Lord listens to me.

Whenever Dad had been especially busy at work, and my sister, brother, and I needed some extra attention, he surprised us with a midnight snack. We would steal away to the kitchen for our favorite ice cream, cookies, or hot chocolate, and lots of good talks. Of course we had to be careful not to wake up Mom, but I'm sure she knew what was going on.

My young son was a reluctant reader and writer. To encourage him, we began interactive journaling. He would write letters to me in his journal, and I would write back to him. I told him that the journal was a safe place to express his thoughts, not a grammar book to be corrected. Our journal opened the door to a magical world of communication where his writing skills rapidly improved and his confidence blossomed.

As a ten-year-old I was devastated when my dog died. My parents framed pictures of my dog and placed them in my room as remembrances. This gesture showed tremendous respect and an understanding of my pain. My parents understood that my grief was real and never treated it as a childhood phase.

My parents celebrated our spiritual birthdays, the dates that we made public decisions to follow Christ and were baptized. We were taught that God had guided our lives since birth, but baptism signified our birth into eternity. Though our chronological birthdays were fun, Mom said that our spiritual birthdays were even more important. Annually each of us had a party to celebrate and renew his or her commitment to God. Gifts ranged from a new Bible, Christian CD, or devotional book to a purity ring. When I went away to college, my parents continued to remember my spiritual birthday and each year sent a gift symbolic of my faith. When my faith was tested at college, this tradition was a positive way for my parents to remind me, without probing questions or lectures, about my commitment to Christ.

Weekly travel means my husband misses all the daily happenings involving our young children. Though he calls often, the children have forgotten by 7:00 P.M.

what they wanted to tell him at 10:00 A.M. To solve the problem, my husband bought a large blank book in which the children can draw pictures for him or write down their thoughts and feelings. We call it "the Daddy book." The children write in it all week, and on Friday nights my husband reads it with them to catch up on what happened while he was away.

Tuesday night was "special plate night" at our house when we were growing up. The plate was actually a decorative bargain plate that we children had selected at a discount store. Each Tuesday a different child used the plate, and everyone else around the table spoke of a quality that they valued in that child. Then we prayed as a family. Year after year the plate rotated around the table, and no matter what conflicts we had had during the day, we affirmed each other with positive comments at night. This custom set the stage for us children to continue to see the best in each other as adults.

I experienced separation issues when I entered kindergarten. Not wanting to leave my mom, I went to school every morning in tears. Mom promised to pray for me three times a day—in the morning, at lunch, and in the afternoon. We set a goal of seven consecutive tear-free days. My reward was a date with Mom at a fancy chocolate shop. After a few weeks we celebrated our sweet success.

Whenever we had to stay home from school because we were ill, our mother brought the "sick basket" out of the closet. It was an old-fashioned latched picnic basket brimming with games, craft supplies, and books that we could only use when we were sick. Every few months she replenished the basket with fresh supplies. It is never fun to be isolated and ill, but the sick basket comforted and distracted us.

My father abandoned our family when my four siblings and I were young children. Mom worked three jobs to support us. Then Mom became fond of a man who had two children of his own. Recognizing that he had a parenting style different from her own and realizing that we children had been through enough changes, she decided to remain single until we were grown. She dated that man for fourteen years—until all of us children were independent. Today they are married and I love my stepfather. Mom sacrificed her own desires to provide a secure home life for us.

My dad made a practice of taking each of us children out for a weekly breakfast date. I liked the idea because he was not distracted by other demands, and we could talk uninterrupted. That breakfast was my hour with him. He took Mom out on dates too.

Mom celebrated our half-birthdays when we were young. She would bake half a cake, give us a card cut in half, and present us with a "half gift," a gift with a critical piece missing. One year Dad received a thermos without a lid. Mom said that life could be too boring, and she loved doing the unexpected. My dad said that she was goofy. She made green eggs and ham for breakfast on Dr. Seuss's birthday. On National Bird Day she made Cornish game hens and we watched Alfred Hitchcock's movie *The Birds*. We ate cherry pie on Presidents' Day and a meatloaf shaped like a groundhog on Groundhog Day. She went completely nuts on major holidays, as our home was filled with relatives and friends. Later I learned that my dad had been raised by a single mom and had experienced a tough childhood. He never met his dad, and his mom had several children fathered by different men. She didn't celebrate my dad's birthday or any other holiday occasions. My mom celebrates not only my dad's birthday, but also his half-birthday and every additional holiday she can think of. Yes, Dad thinks that she is goofy, but he feels very loved. No one can make up for a lost childhood, but my mom comes close.

We had a simple rule in our family when we were growing up: one put-down equals two "put-ups." If we criticized a family member, we were required to offer two compliments or affirming statements for every negative comment we had made.

My mom kept a surprise bag handy for any unpleasant experiences such as long trips, visits to the dentist, or anything else that I dreaded. Whether we were in the car for hours or in a doctor's waiting room, the surprise bag helped ease my frustration and calm my anxiety. Today as an adult I try to associate a pleasant experience with an unpleasant task.

As an adopted child, I could have felt second best. Instead my parents made me feel twice as special. Instead of letting me feel that my life was fragmented, they gave me two birthday parties each year, one on my chronological birthday and another on the day they legally adopted me. My parents celebrated the fact that I was a precious gift to them. They said that I should have two birthdays a year because, having two sets of parents, I was twice loved. Their theme of "double love" was my foundation when other children asked me hurtful questions about my real parents and when I wondered about my roots.

Mom worked hard to be an anchor of stability after my dad left. She would tell us, "We are still a family." We continued our family devotions, mealtime and bedtime rituals, and holiday celebrations. In the midst of the chaos, Mom affirmed that we could still count on our family.

When we were children, Dad traveled all week and returned to mountains of paperwork on the weekends. As he worked in his study, Mom would close his door to give him peace and quiet. But Dad always opened the door so we could run in to talk with him, hug him, or just sit next to him. Our dad modeled how our heavenly Father loves us and is always available.

When I was in junior high school, Mom and I had an informal pact. When she picked me up after school, if I had had a bad day or had forgotten my lunch, she would stop at my favorite fast-food restaurant or deli sandwich shop on the way home. I was allowed one such treat each week. This "treat of the week" gave me something to look forward to during a tough day.

Mom said we should do the most important things first. Every week the two of us brought home a bundle of books from the library. We began each day drinking hot chocolate while reading the Bible and our library books. Since our reading time was from 7:00 A.M. to 9:00 A.M., we were never disturbed by phone calls or other interruptions. As a journalism major today, I continue to have a passion for literature and writing. My love for the written word started early in life. More important, I knew that my mom made spending time and sharing books with me a priority.

Being a middle child is not easy. Since I was born between an overachieving older sister and a cute little brother, my parents made an extra effort to make me feel special. They told me that I was the sweet cream in the middle of the cookie. (My sister once told me that what is really in the middle of the cookie is lard—pig fat! But I love her anyway.) When asked how many children she had, my mom would answer, "Three *only* children." My parents treated us as individuals, each with unique gifts and talents.

When my mom traveled, she would leave chocolate kisses for us to find throughout the house during her absence. Those yummy treats reminded us that Mom was thinking of us.

No matter what problems we had during the day, our family reserved dinnertime as the conflict-free hour. Mom kept jars filled with slips of paper near the dining table. One jar held prayers and Scripture verses for the blessing. Another jar held the "How Was Your Day?" game. Passing that jar around the table, we pulled out slips of paper and read questions like "When did you laugh the hardest today?" or "When were you maddest today?" or "What was the silliest thing you said today?" Thinking up questions to keep in that jar was as much fun as answering them. Aside from this game, when Mom asked us, "What did you do today?" we usually responded, "Nothing." Another jar held slips of paper listing after-dinner activities such as card games, sing-alongs, or going out for ice cream. Dinnertime was physically and emotionally nourishing.

Whenever we leave on a trip or go to camp, Mom hides treats and letters in our bags. There is one surprise for each day of the trip. She does the same thing for my dad when he travels on business.

On a bad day when I didn't feel like praying, Mom made bedtime prayers easy. She encouraged me to share with God "one grateful and one grumbly." I could usually think of at least one thing to thank God for and then I could tell him about my bad day. Mom listened and helped me understand that God was listening too.

When I was growing up, every year I received a birth-day wreath decorated with ornaments symbolizing landmark events, accomplishments, and obstacles I had overcome. Usually the wreath had twelve ornaments, one for each of the twelve months of the past year. Whenever I struggled with a task, my parents would encourage me by saying, "Now that will need a place on your birthday wreath this year." I earned a music ornament when I completed a difficult song on the piano, and a miniature soccer ball when I finished the soccer season even though I was one of the worst players on the team. Because I had learning problems, I did not receive affirmation at school or from my peers, but I was motivated to try my best because of those ornaments which were symbolic of my parents' belief in me.

As soon as I could hold up three fingers, my mother taught me sign language for "I love you." Holding up a thumb, first finger, and little finger became a secret message that she could communicate across a room when I was happy, sad, anxious, or frightened. She would flash her sign to me from the audience when I was nervous during a church or school musical performance. Though I am now an adult, we still say hello and goodbye with our "I love you" sign. In a stressful situation she comforts me with that reassuring tradition.

All your sons will be taught by the Lord,
and great will be your children's peace.

ISAIAH 54:13

CHAPTER

6

What to Do When You Don't Know What to Say to . . . Your Teenagers

Therefore encourage one another and build each other up, just as in fact you are doing.

1 THESSALONIANS 5:11

Teenagers tend to live on the edge and experience unusual stress in life. When one of my teenagers explodes at me in the morning before leaving for school, I try to remember the pressures I endured as a busy teen including mountains of homework, numerous extracurricular activities, overwhelming college applications, and social dilemmas. My response varies. For one daughter, I cook "make-up pasta" for dinner. For another daughter, I have brownies waiting when she returns from school or leave her favorite shampoo on her desk. Though their bedrooms are normally their sole responsibility, when they are returning from a trip I make their beds with clean linen, turn back their sheets, and put welcome-home signs on their pillows.

Throughout my years in high school, my dad helped me with my math homework. He purchased a copy of my math textbook to take with him on business trips. As we talked by phone, he followed along in the text and walked me through the complicated equations. When I became frustrated, my dad helped and encouraged me even when he was across the country. Sometimes I called him at 10:00 P.M. West Coast time, not realizing it was 1:00 A.M. where he was on the East Coast. Though I woke him from a sound sleep, he never complained.

It wasn't what my parents did on Sunday morning that affected my faith. It was what they did Monday through Saturday that reinforced my belief in Jesus

Christ. My parents never held us children to standards that they did not live up to themselves. Teens watch their parents carefully to see if their faith is real in daily life or merely words.

I plan lunch dates with my friends, so why not plan such events with my children? Dates with my daughters began as monthly mother-daughter dinners away from the distractions of telephone and TV. Dates with my son began with having breakfast out. Time with my children has expanded and diversified to taking an exercise class together, going for long walks, attending plays and concerts, or even playing laser tag. We finish the evening with dessert. During these dates we have enjoyed many serious discussions, not forced by the heat of the moment. By building relationships now, I can look forward to being friends with my children when they are adults.

All teenagers need mentors and good role models in their lives. Teens who have stopped listening to their parents will often listen to mentors. Even teens who come from the healthiest of families and have good relationships with their parents need other adults to help them negotiate the challenges of adolescence. One of my daughters' mentors is their dance instructor. She is an excellent teacher who not only passes on the skills and love of dancing to my daughters, but also patiently listens to them. Besides seeing my girls four nights a week, she sometimes attends dance movies with them. This teacher offers her students a safe place to vent their frustrations with school problems or relationship issues and offers advice when asked. I am grateful to every teacher, coach, and youth leader who has taken the time to listen to my children. I have had the privilege of spending hours talking with many of my children's friends; I call them my adopted children. As parents we can encourage our children to have mentor relationships, and we can provide a safe place for other young people.

My parents completely embraced and supported my passions. They never missed one of my soccer games. On the morning before a game, there was always a soccer ball candle on my breakfast plate. Through the years my mom sewed my jerseys into a quilt representing all the teams for which I played. My pursuits have changed through the years, but my parents' interest has never wavered. They are my most enthusiastic cheerleaders.

After church our family enjoyed Sunday dinner while we discussed the morning's sermon. Our parents asked, "What was the most important thing you learned today?" or "What Scripture verse spoke to you?" We summed up what we learned on an index card and put it on the refrigerator as a reminder for the week. This practice developed a lifelong habit that helped us apply what we learned during worship time to real-life problems.

My mother could no longer help me with my homework when I was placed in high school honors classes, but she stayed up with me while I studied. She often brushed my hair to keep me awake. Those head massages and her company eased the stress of a heavy school load. Her support made all the difference. She wanted me to have every opportunity that she did not have as a teenager and spent her savings to send me to an excellent college.

When we were teenagers, my dad took my brothers and me on camping trips every summer. Without TV, Nintendo, and other distractions, we talked about everything we were facing at different stages of our lives. I realize now that the greatest gift that my dad gave us was his uninterrupted *time*.

My parents and my friends' parents were quite involved in our high school life. My mom would often have food waiting for my friends and me to devour when we came home during our forty-minute lunch break. She set the table, complete with candles, and picked up Chinese food, pizza, or another favorite take-out meal. A friend's mom regularly hosted the pre-dance reception before homecoming or prom events. Twenty teenagers and their parents gathered to pin corsages, take group pictures, make videotapes, and help with final touches. We also enjoyed mother-daughter shopping days. I felt supported by my own parents and by my friends' parents. They made a conscious effort to stand united and be involved in our lives. Everyone kept a watchful eye.

"Comfort food" can send messages of encouragement where words fail. Whenever my second born teenage daughter has a tough week or needs some extra family loving, I serve a mock Thanksgiving dinner. Most important to her are the cranberry sauce and mashed potatoes. My oldest daughter associates chocolate-chip scones with life's special events. She looked forward to having scones on the first day of every school year, and now she counts on finding scones waiting for her on the kitchen counter when she returns home from college for holiday visits.

My parents gave me a purity ring on my fifteenth birthday and encouraged me to sign a purity contract to abstain from sex until marriage. They followed the same custom when each of my sisters and brothers turned fifteen. My parents expanded the purity concept to include abstaining from drugs, alcohol, and any behaviors that would jeopardize our safety or cause deep regret later in life. The theme of our contracts was that we were daughters and sons of the King, and we should therefore develop a "royal" lifestyle. Included with our birthday contracts, which were written in Old English script, were celebratory letters from mentors, relatives, and close friends who also encouraged us in our purity journey. Some friends shared joyful experiences and explained why they were glad they had abstained. Others described the consequences of poor choices. Knowing that we have many caring people supporting us in our desire to obey God and live a life without regrets, my siblings and I continue to wear our purity rings.

Mom was a great listener who rarely gave unrequested advice. When I returned from school, I sometimes found a candy bar she had left for me, but I also often found a relevant Scripture verse taped to my computer screen with a note saying she had prayed for me that day. She called prayers "spiritual hugs." Whether I had a tough test or a problem with a friend, I knew Mom was with me in prayer.

My parents encouraged us to reach out to others. One Christmas we went with our church family to serve food in a soup kitchen. Another year we collected gifts for needy families. During the summer our youth choir, led by my dad, performed at churches for the homeless. Throughout the year our family sent money to support children in impoverished countries. I grew up seeing their pictures and letters on our refrigerator. When I was an eighteen-year-old student teacher, one of my students came from an abused family. The week before Christmas I learned that a boyfriend had beaten his mother. She couldn't afford to buy Christmas presents for her children. With donations from my parents and grandmother, I purchased the scooter I knew my student dreamed of and delivered it to his home on Christmas Eve. I will never forget his ecstatic response. My parents taught me that one person can make a difference, and it is truly more rewarding to give than to receive.

Late at night, when I am tired and yearning for bed, is the time that my teenagers most want to talk about their concerns. As they begin to open up, I ignore the clock and give them my full attention. I also invest in cell phones so that my teens can talk to me at any time. They won't be teens very long, and I don't want to miss a minute of opportunity to keep our communication lines open and our relationship strong as they begin the transition to young adulthood.

To celebrate my entrance into adolescence, my mom took me on a weekend trip to the beach (away from my siblings). We discussed the physical and emotional changes I would face and my mom provided a safe place for me to ask any questions. She wove in encouraging devotional materials. We had a wonderful time, and I returned home feeling cherished and prepared for the future.

At a Christian conference the speaker/counselor roared with laughter when a mother in the audience asked, "What should I do about my daughter's messy room?

This is our big issue. She refuses to keep it clean. Our God is a God of order and I know that cleanliness is next to godliness." The speaker pointed out that the messy room was actually the mother's problem, not the daughter's problem. He advised, "Pick your battles carefully. Never argue about clothes, appearance, or a clean room. If it is not an issue critical to character development, drop it." If I daily nag my teens about little things, they tune me out. Then they are not listening when the time comes to discuss important issues.

With three children going to school and participating in church activities, and Mom and Dad maintaining their careers, we were a busy household. But our parents made our yearly family vacation a priority. Funds were limited, but their philosophy was that while we could get along with an older couch for another year, we couldn't miss a chance to build vacation memories—childhood was so short. Mom and Dad also took me out of school for a "mental health day" every year. On that day my parents gave me their full attention while we slipped off on a day trip to someplace exciting.

My parents were firm believers in rites of passage. On each birthday I received one added privilege and one added responsibility. For example, when I turned sixteen I received my driver's license and access to the car, but was required to save one afternoon a week for running errands for Mom. My parents spelled out their guidelines in contracts. I read each contract and signed it if I agreed to the terms. I signed driving contracts, purity contracts, and baby-sitting contracts. Whenever a disagreement arose, we returned to the contract to clarify any confusion. To celebrate rites of passage my parents created fun gifts for my siblings and me. When my sister left home, she received a cookbook filled with all of Mom's best recipes and holiday traditions. My brother was given a quilt made of twelve years of his baseball jerseys stitched together. My gift was a quilt of fabric squares taken from my favorite childhood holiday dresses. In addition, we were given journals filled with letters our parents had written on our birthdays detailing our annual festivities, milestone events, and affirming how much we were loved.

Life is the first gift, love is the second,
and understanding the third.

MARGIE PIERCY

CHAPTER

7

What to Do When You Don't Know What to Say to . . . Your Struggling Teens

Fathers, do not embitter your children, or they will become discouraged.

COLOSSIANS 3:21

Dad's job demanded that he travel often. As I entered adolescence, I became an angry, rebellious teenager. After one unusually difficult day my mom telephoned my dad to discuss my behavior. Instead of getting angry with me, my dad quit his job, took a different position that did not require him to travel, and relocated our family to a quieter community. He gave up his career to spend my teenage years with me because he valued me more than financial gain and prestige. His actions said "I love you" louder than any words.

The best thing my parents did for my faith was to emphasize character over appearance. I'm sure that when my siblings and I went to church, we often embarrassed them with our dyed hair, pierced bodies, and clothes that were on the edge of being inappropriate. Yet our parents didn't try to put our faith in a box. They valued us above their own reputation and what other people thought. That took a lot of courage.

As a women's retreat speaker I counseled countless individuals about their broken backgrounds and poor life choices. I found it easy to love unconditionally and offer compassion to other people. My greatest test came when my own young adult daughter made poor choices and suffered the consequences. My immediate response was that she should have known better. Then I realized that she needed my love and acceptance, not my judgment. Why would I offer more compassion to a total stranger than to my own daughter?

I was a gangly, unattractive thirteen-year-old from a broken home. My self-esteem was at its lowest point when in eighth grade I injured my leg and had to use crutches. Since I was unable to participate in my physical education class, a school counselor asked if I would work as her aide during that free hour. Each day I hobbled to her office where she had assignments for me to correct and papers to file. She complimented my work, genuinely enjoyed my presence, remembered me with gifts on holidays, and kept the bottom drawer of her desk supplied with snacks for me. Looking back, I appreciate how this counselor saw past my outward appearance to a diamond in the rough. She gave me a feeling of usefulness and confidence, and provided the stability that a teenager with a chaotic home life needed.

When I was sent to jail for being in a car with friends who were involved in a robbery, my parents didn't rescue me or bail me out, but neither did they abandon me. They visited me as often as possible. Though I had attended church with my parents for years, I hadn't paid much attention. Once in jail, however, I participated in the chaplain's Bible study and talked to my parents about what I had learned. They patiently listened and loved me even while I was in prison.

A suicidal young man became obsessed with our teenage daughter. They both attended the same high school, and we had reason to be concerned about our daughter's physical safety as well as that of her boyfriend. Removing her from school was not the answer because school was the center of her very active social and academic life. Though we tried, we realized we could not watch her twenty-four hours a day. Besides, the young man was a karate expert, and we were no match for him. Then an incredible thing happened. Our daughter's Christian friends, as well as our friends from church and in the community, helped us keep watch. She was constantly surrounded and never alone. Adults who worked at her school consistently supervised her. Her school counselor, who attended our church, guided our daughter through the entire experience and helped the young man obtain the help he needed. Through this incident our daughter gained important skills for coping with a crisis. My maternal instinct is to shield my children from any pain, to stop any crisis before it happens. I learned that my job as a parent is not to protect my children from pain, but to guide them safely through painful experiences. I think that God our Father uses the same method!

My parents were church addicts, attending Bible studies, choir rehearsals, and committee meetings nearly every night of the week. They participated in church cleanup days on Saturdays and spent the entire day at church on Sundays. As a young adult I learned that this addiction can result in what is called "church orphan syndrome." My mother and father were as uninvolved with their family as alcoholics who go to bars every night. My parents' addiction was different, but more insidious.

At birth I was adopted into a wonderful family. My adoptive parents made every effort to stay in contact with my birth mother and her parents. Though this contact may sometimes be painful for my adopted parents, I am grateful to have a second family who loves me. My birth mother and grandparents care about me and are available to answer my questions. True love does not feel threatened. My wise adoptive parents widened the circle of love around me.

Fifty years ago my teenage son lay dying of leukemia. While visiting him in the hospital, some people from church stated that they were concerned about his salvation because he had long hair. I never returned to that church. When my son died, I know that the gates of heaven opened wide to receive him, and no one measured his hair.

When my daughter was fifteen years old, she became involved with an abusive boyfriend. He even threatened to kill her. Because their relationship began normally, then deteriorated over time, it was difficult to see the abuse coming. She was already bonded to him, so my husband and I knew that forbidding the relationship would only fuel the fire. I began doing research about abusive relationships and daily shared bits of information with her. We gently loved her and talked openly. When she was ready, I met alone with the boy in a public park, and we discussed his destructive behavior. I made it clear that we cared about him and prayed for him, but the relationship with our daughter was over. He did not pursue her again. Bombarding our daughter with rules and research would have alienated her. The key to helping was to listen to her and gradually welcome her back.

I was confused and looking for direction in my life. I didn't have an answer to that age-old question, What do you want to do when you grow up? My mom would say, "The question is not, What do you want to do when you grow up? The question is, What do you want to do next?" When I explored gardening, she put me in charge of her flower and vegetable gardens. When I considered interior design, she gave me furniture to refinish and rooms to redecorate. She gave me real opportunities to try my hand at everything. She cut the electrical cord off broken appliances and let me take them apart. She paid local craftsmen to teach me basic construction, basic mechanics, and basic electrical skills. Our home reflected the interests of our family members, filled with 4-H projects, computers, a spinning wheel, a weaving loom, a sewing machine, bookcases, a painting easel, musical instruments, horses, dogs, and birds. Mom's motto was that our home was an art studio for budding artists.

Without fail, our family attended every service offered at our church. It never occurred to me that church attendance was optional. My parents had a sincere faith in Christ, but they were unhappy with their relationship and with themselves. My father was an especially harsh man. Appearances and unquestioning obedience were important to him. Shoes had to be shined to perfection. When I was a teenager, he thought my hair was too long and cut it off while I was sleeping. Desperately trying to please him, I did chores without being asked. Once, after I swept the garage, he responded, "Do it over. It's not clean enough." Nothing I did was ever perfect enough. Dad was equally hard on my mother. It is surprising that I didn't rebel against him and God. Later I even went to seminary and became a pastor. Though they struggled in their marriage, my parents remained committed to each other for a lifetime. Their lives were far from perfect, but their faith was real.

When our teenage daughter told us that she was pregnant, we simply held her and cried with her. There wasn't anything that needed to be said except "We love you and you are not alone."

Anytime I was grounded, my parents curtailed all my high school social activities and required my attendance at more church functions. A week of grounding meant attending Sunday school, Bible study, and youth group. My parents meant well, but I learned to associate being punished with going to church. Spending time with God meant not spending time with my friends. As an adult, it has been difficult for me to separate God's love from punishment.

When our daughter in college began making choices with which we did not agree, I realized that the most important thing was to keep the lines of communication open. We could not influence her if we didn't have a relationship with her. Continuing a supportive, loving relationship with our daughter became the focus. Being available to talk and staying in frequent contact with her helped ease her transition to adulthood.

My parents died in an accident when I was a preschooler. The family who took me in cared for my physical needs, but nothing more. They never attended my Little League games. I went to the ball field alone for every practice and game. When I was fourteen years old, my coach said, "With your background, it would be easy to get into trouble. I'm impressed that you haven't taken that path. I'm proud of you." Today at forty-four I still hear those affirming words. For the past thirty years I have wanted to live up to my coach's belief in a lonely teen.

Growing up in a loving Christian family, I developed a strong faith in God. I married a solid Christian man, and we entered a life of ministry. Though raised in the same home, my brother turned his back on God during high school and never returned. There are no magic formulas for raising children. The best gifts we can give them are a solid community of faith and a supportive church family. Teenagers need adults to encourage and guide them. Parents cannot do this alone. Mentor relationships must be in place before teens hit their rebellious years. When our daughter was starting to question her faith, she began dating a non-Christian young man. We voiced our concerns, but she tuned us out. My friend, who had already established a relationship with our daughter, took her out for coffee and shared biblical truths, but never judged her or told her what to do. When our daughter broke off the relationship with her boyfriend, my friend knew how traumatic this experience was and said, "I will be sleeping by the phone. You can call me anytime." With a new baby, my friend wasn't getting enough sleep as it was, yet she was available to our daughter day and night. When our daughter would not listen to us, my friend walked her through the difficult journey.

My dad showed little interest in my brothers and me after he divorced our mom. Then Dad remarried and his new wife, who also had a son, decided that we were going to be part of the family. She included us in trips and holiday events. Knowing about my love for horses, she encouraged me to enter competitions that she and my dad attended. I could not afford to attend college, so my stepmom researched all the animal-trainer programs in the state and helped me fill out the required applications. My new mom became my champion.

Our parents, pillars of the church, gave time and money to good causes. However, as teenagers we learned that while supporting causes to help broken people was commendable, associating with them was unacceptable. Our parents taught us to make this distinction because they did not want us to be tainted by questionable behavior. They gave money to a program for homeless drug addicts, but when my high school friend was hospitalized for alcohol poisoning, I wasn't allowed to have contact with him again. Our church gave donations to a crisis pregnancy center for unwed teenagers, but when a girl in our youth group became pregnant, the silent disapproval of other church members drove her and her family from our congregation. As an adult I realize that my parents were afraid, but there is no place for fear in the gospel of Christ. Jesus came to heal the broken, and we are privileged to be his tangible hands in the process. Loving the broken should be modeled for young people. Firsthand experience, with supervision, should be encouraged.

My shy son hated attending church. A quiet junior high student, he didn't like big parties or events (or girls), and he did not want to participate in our youth group. My son did love to play baseball, however. Observing that there were other young teenage boys like my son in our community, a Christian college student informally invited them to come to church on Thursday evenings to play baseball or basketball. Amazingly, my son agreed to go and even brought friends with him. This wise college student included a short devotional series in the Thursday evening program. He initially intended this activity to be an outreach to the community, but it was also an "in reach" to church kids. Like Jesus, he went to the people and valued their individual interests and needs.

The best thing my parents did was to allow me to develop my own faith. While I was a teenager, my parents never made church attendance a condition of living at home as my friends' parents did. Sometimes I wanted to sleep in on Sunday mornings. Rather than force the issue, they suggested that I read the Bible and pray later in the day. My parents felt that it was important for me to attend church, though not necessarily theirs. They encouraged me to attend other Christian churches and camps with my high school friends. We were a prominent family in our church, and I know that my sporadic attendance was noticed. Sometimes the youth leaders made critical comments. While I was still in high school, my faith became my own, independent of my family. I became an advocate for abstinence and arranged for a speaker to come to my school and speak on the subject. During college I was involved with Campus Crusade and campus Bible studies and worked as a counselor at a Christian summer camp. As an adult I am a committed Christian. If my parents had made church attendance an issue like cleaning my room or observing curfews, I probably would have viewed God as another set of rules and rebelled. Instead I learned that I had an individual relationship with God.

You paved the road for me, but let me make my own journey.

VIRGINIA REYNOLDS

CHAPTER

8

What to Do When You Don't Know What to Say to . . . Your Adult Children

Do not let any unwholesome talk come out of your mouths, but only what is helpful for building others up according to their needs, that it may benefit those who listen.

EPHESIANS 4:29

As a college freshman, I am immersed in a busy new lifestyle. I don't call home as often as I should, but my mom regularly sends me encouraging cards with special treats tucked inside—gum, socks, coffee, ice cream certificates, quarters for the laundry, Post-it notes, hot-chocolate packets, candy, or pens. This caring gesture makes me feel loved and mothered as I strive for independence. Every college student loves to receive mail.

When my husband was sent to prison for molesting our daughters, my parents stepped in to help. They paid my rent for eighteen months so that we did not have to move and experience more chaos. Because of them I was able to attend college and pursue a career. They have faithfully stood by me during this devastating crisis. Today I can support my children because of my parents' financial help.

My husband's parents believe in staying connected as a family. They regularly plan reunions and trips for their four adult children, including spouses and grandchildren. We have enjoyed relaxing vacations at the lake and cruises to exciting places. Their generosity has created a bond of friendship between sons and daughters, sons-in-law and daughters-in-law, and cousins. After my husband's father died, his mother continued these celebrations with her children. This is her legacy.

Every day I was in the military I received something in the mail from my father. Having been in the military himself, Dad said he never wanted me to walk away from mail call empty-handed. When duty took me away from the base, I would return to a stack of mail from home. Presently my own son is in the military overseas. Every day I send him a letter and enclose comics to make him smile. I never want him to walk away from mail call empty-handed.

The night my husband proposed to me, I went home crying and confused because he was handicapped and confined to a wheelchair. My mother assured me that she had faithfully prayed that my future husband would be a godly man with integrity, honesty, and strong faith. She had prayed that he would be a faithful partner, loving husband, and tender father. She held me and said that she had never prayed about his legs. She encouraged me to see that all his amazing qualities were far more important than a perfect physical body and gave me permission to follow my heart. Mom gave us her blessing, and she has been my husband's biggest fan.

During a financial crisis there was just not enough money to make ends meet for my husband, our four small children, and myself. My mother and mother-in-law helped by asking, prior to birthdays and gift-giving holidays, what gifts would be the most useful. They made the extra effort to partner with us and use their gift-giving funds to provide for such needs as shoes and coats for the children, school supplies, car repairs, a family zoo pass, and library cards. Our mothers were on our team as we struggled through a bleak time.

When I went across the country to college, I was not homesick until Sunday afternoon. I missed our family dinners after church and the lively conversations. My parents recorded their Sunday dinners and mailed a tape to me every Monday. Each part of the tape was comforting from the opening blessing to the arguments between my siblings to the news about the past week or upcoming events. Sometimes my family would talk to me as if I were sitting at the table with them. Those tapes were the highlight of my week and made me feel connected to my family.

When I became seriously ill due to postsurgical complications, my parents dropped everything and traveled to be by my side. The ordeal extended into months, and my parents took turns leaving their full-time jobs to take care of me and transport me to medical appointments. I realize now that I could have died from serious infections that did not respond to treatment. My parents put their lives on hold to care for me during this critical time.

While my sister and I were schoolchildren, Mom tucked Bible verses in the lunches she packed for us. When we went away to college, she e-mailed us every morning. Sometimes she would send Bible verses, quotes, or song lyrics during the crisis of the week. Now that my sister has graduated and has a demanding job, Mom continues to e-mail words of encouragement. Mom's efforts tell us two things: (1) she thinks about us and prays for us daily, and (2) she takes the time to find out what is happening in our lives and is always there to support us.

I doubt that I will ever experience the empty nest. Developmentally disabled, my forty-year-old adult son works in a shelter during the day but resides in my home. After my husband died, my son's presence was a great comfort. Daily my son gives me hugs and kisses, and helps me with the mundane chores of the home. Though I did not give birth to a "normal" son forty years ago, he is a priceless blessing in my life.

I missed my mom's silly holiday traditions when I went away to college. Our Valentine tradition was that family members would draw names on February 1, surprise those secret pals with gifts through February 14, and write funny poems to reveal who our secret pals were on Valentine's Day. One February I had experienced a bad week at college where I was a theater major. In addition to being homesick, I had received one too many audition rejections and was questioning the direction of my life. Then a package arrived filled with a variety of secret pal gifts from my parents and siblings. They had not forgotten me, and since I could not join them for the holiday fun, they had sent the fun to me. Across the miles I was still part of my crazy family.

My daughter and I share a passion for literature and writing. While she was in high school, I regularly helped her brainstorm about homework projects. I was her sounding board and often her loving critic/editor. It was a privilege to be invited into her thought processes. When she left for college, I knew how much I would miss those sessions. Then my daughter started calling to discuss assignments and e-mailing her papers to me. I wondered if I should still be proofreading her papers, though I found very few errors and didn't have much to contribute. Then a good friend said, "Don't you see? She still wants you to be her audience. She wants to stay connected and share her thoughts with you." No matter how late at night my daughter calls, I am grateful for that contact.

Months of agonizing tests revealed that my husband and I were unable to conceive a baby without expensive medical intervention. The cost took our breath away. Without hesitation, my parents paid for the entire process. Our son is a miracle, born of the generosity and love of his grandparents.

At 12:30 A.M. the phone rang, waking us out of a sound sleep. My daughter, a college student, called to tell us that another student had gone on a killing rampage with his car on a street near her apartment. The suspect was intoxicated and mentally unstable. Having been at the scene of the accident, my daughter had covered one body with her coat and given CPR to another victim. Four students had been killed and one seriously injured. Two of the students were my daughter's close friends. Our first reaction was to bring our daughter home, but she needed to stay and talk to the police, and she wanted to remain with the other grieving coeds. We decided to go to her. We packed at

1:00 A.M. and drove six hours to reach her by dawn. We sat on the floor of my daughter's apartment and listened as she and her friends talked about the incident. As a doer, I wanted to *do* something like clean her apartment or help with laundry. But she just wanted me to listen. We spent the weekend with her. My advice to parents whose child has experienced a traumatic event is simple: *Go.*

I was living across the country from my parents when my marriage fell apart. My mother sent me prepaid phone cards so I could call family and friends whenever I needed to talk to someone. Her gifts eased my feelings of loneliness and isolation by connecting me with those who loved and supported me.

My mother kept a journal while she was pregnant with me. Sometimes she wrote about her pregnancy and changing body; other times she wrote letters to me, her unborn child. She gave this journal to me when I was pregnant with my first child. I read about her journey as I took my own.

When my husband was transferred to another state, the most difficult part of moving was leaving my parents.

Arriving at our new home, I was comforted to find a letter from my parents in the mailbox. Through the following months, my parents continued to send care packages with favorite foods that we could not find in our new setting. Every week we made special meals with these favorite flavors and talked with our children about cherished memories. They were missing their grandparents as much as we were. My parents did not allow distance to interfere with our relationship.

I married my husband against my mother's advice. My mom was deeply hurt when I turned my back on her. She was also concerned about my safety because I chose a career in law enforcement. I viewed her questions as constant disapproval and severed our relationship. Later when I was divorced and my career choice required that I attend a six-week training session out of state, my mother came to care for my children in my home. She demonstrated in concrete ways that her love was unconditional. She supported me even when she did not agree with my life decisions.

The week after I moved into my college dorm room I received a package in the mail from my mother. When I opened the package, a pair of freshly starched and pressed apron strings fell out. My mother's letter said she was proud of the man I had become, and she knew I would continue to do well in my life as an adult.

My husband passed on his love of adventure to our children. When they were young, he often said, "Let's go find an adventure." Saturday was "Daddy Day" and our children never knew what spontaneous excursion awaited them. As our children matured into teens and young adults, the local adventures evolved into trips around the country and the world. My husband takes our children on individual birthday adventures ranging from scuba diving, skiing, fishing, or golfing trips to symphony concerts and backstage visits to the Grand Old Opry. My husband never runs out of ideas for his adventure buddies.

I was extremely upset when our young adult daughter told us that she was dating an older, divorced man who was not a Christian. My husband wisely reminded me that we had always welcomed our children's friends into our home. As difficult as it was for me, we invited our daughter's boyfriend to visit us whenever our daughter did. As the years passed, we have grown to love this man and understand why our daughter cares for him. If we had taken a stand and not welcomed him into our home and lives, we would have alienated our daughter and missed the opportunity to show unconditional love to this man.

Ever since I left home, my parents have called me on my birthday at 12:05 A.M., the exact time that I was born. They have told me that they call to remember the exact moment they "received a priceless gift, the moment they became parents and their lives changed in the most incredible, miraculous way." They are the first people to wish me happy birthday and remind me how extraordinary I am to them.

Putting the final touches on my college senior design project, I realized I had left an important illustration board at my parents' home across the state. I telephoned Mom before she left for church and asked if she could bring the board and meet me halfway. Instead Mom drove with my project all the way to my college. She arrived before my presentation and stayed to help me pack up my dorm room while I took finals. This is my Mom, who goes all the way, not halfway, for me.

After being my cheery companion for eight years, my Yorkshire terrier died unexpectedly. She was my baby, the center of my home. My father, who lives in another state, called me almost every day for several weeks to check on me. Though not an animal lover himself, he understood that my grief was genuine. He compassionately listened and validated my feelings by saying, "It's natural for you to feel this way right now. I wish that I could be there to hold you."

I was attending a prestigious college in another state when I was dismissed for breaking the rules. My parents had been proud of me when I had been accepted for admission. Dreading their reaction, I slowly made my way home. As I drove down our long driveway, I saw Mom and Dad standing on the front porch waiting for me. My parents hugged me and welcomed me home. Their love and acceptance set the stage for me to make better choices in the future.

When I was out of the country on mission trips or with the military, my parents sent me packets of Kool-aid to make the water I had to drink taste better. They sent vegetable seeds, combs, toothpaste, toothbrushes, socks, emery boards, band-aids, and headache relievers. Each carefully thought-out package was exactly what I needed and assured me I was in my parents' prayers.

My husband has held twenty jobs in our dozen years of marriage. My parents have loved and supported us, often sending checks even when doing so meant that they would have a financially tight month. Mom and Dad could probably have retired by now if they had not helped us. They have a wonderful relationship with my husband and children. They give with no strings attached.

My two sons are attending different colleges away from home. To keep in touch, I logged onto a "yellow pages" site on the internet and typed in the name of each college to find a list of businesses near each campus. With this information I buy gift cards from a variety of stores and restaurants within walking distance of the campuses since my sons do not own cars. For the money I would spend on postage for heavy care packages, I send gift cards to my sons throughout the year. They love to receive these mailbox coupons.

As an unwed teenager I gave birth to a daughter. I never married her father, an angry young man who ended up with a jail sentence. My parents supported me as I attended school in order to develop a solid career. They have cared for my daughter as their own, and I can see her as frequently as I like. Through all the changes in my own life, they have given my daughter a stable, loving home life.

On my first birthday away from home I was attending college in another state, far from my family and friends. My mom surprised me by creating a computer web page. All my relatives and friends sent birthday wishes and photos to greet me when I checked my e-mail on my birthday.

Whenever I face challenging circumstances or life's closed doors, I remember my mom's words: "What has God put in my hand to do?" Mom has been my example, my compass. Taking stock of a situation, she asks God what lies within her realm of influence and what he has placed in her stewardship. Her words have become my motto. She trusts God without being a victim. I learned from Mom that there is true freedom in carefully tending to what God has placed in my hands and leaving the rest to him.

You may let me out of your sight,
but never out of your heart.
VIRGINIA REYNOLDS

SECTION III

Extended Family

*Near the cross of Jesus stood his mother, his
mother's sister, Mary the wife of Clopas, and
Mary Magdalene. When Jesus saw his
mother there, and the disciple whom he loved
standing nearby, he said to his mother, "Dear
woman, here is your son," and to the disciple, "Here is your mother." From that time
on, this disciple took her into his home.*

JOHN 19:25–27

God understood the importance of the par-
ent-child relationship. One of Christ's last
gestures was to provide for his mother. As he
hung dying on the cross, he entrusted John with
her care.

God directs us to honor our parents. He didn't say, "Honor your parents if they have done an outstanding job." We are to honor, to respect, our parents and those who have come before us in our lineages.

Mary Ann's friend was physically, emotionally, and sexually abused by her parents. Her childhood was a nightmare. Yet as a healed Christian who understood that forgiveness is the heart of the gospel, she returned home to offer love and forgiveness to her parents before they died. She even scrubbed her mother's home until it was spotless. This friend honored her parents though they had caused her great pain.

In this section you will discover tangible ways to love and honor your parents, in-laws, grandparents, aunts, uncles, and other extended family members. You will also find ideas for nurturing your siblings.

Let us not become conceited, provoking and envying each other.

GALATIANS 5:26

What to Do When You Don't Know What to Say to . . . Your Own Parents

Honor your father and your mother, as the Lord your God has commanded you, so that you may live long and that it may go well with you in the land the Lord your God is giving you.

DEUTERONOMY 5:16

My parents are no longer able to drive, so I take them to the bank, the market, and medical appointments. As well as looking after my parents, I am shuttling my children to a myriad of activities. Whenever I feel pressed for time, I remember the countless rides my parents gave me to school, music lessons, and friends' houses. The score will never be even; I will always be gratefully in their debt. When I am in my eighties, I hope that my children will cheerfully offer me rides.

After my husband moved out, my young adult son threw a birthday party for me and invited all my friends. My son loves to cook and has continued to plan countless events in honor of holidays and birthdays. He showed me that our social life did not end when his dad, and my husband, left.

Though my parents were neglectful and abusive, I continue to remember them on holidays and throughout the year by sending simple but thoughtful cards and gifts. While I am careful to avoid situations that are hurtful to me, I choose to have as much of a relationship as our sticky situation will allow. Spending holidays together is unthinkable, but occasional e-mails and gifts of magazine subscriptions, cheerful books, pleasant videos, and uplifting music keep a bridge between us.

My husband and I are no longer able to travel as we once did. We used to spend every summer vacation on the coast of Nova Scotia, but failing health has put an end to our visits. For our fiftieth wedding anniversary our daughter and her husband came across the country to push our wheelchairs through the airport and take us on a final trip to that beautiful coastline.

My youngest son continued to live at home after my husband died. When I fell and broke my neck, I would have been forced to move to a skilled nursing facility if he had not been there to help me. He cares for me and looks after the car and home maintenance projects. His friends bring life into the house. His willingness to remain at home during my recovery allowed me to keep my independence.

As children, my neighbor and I were best friends and our mothers were equally close. Even relocating across the state did not change our relationship. Decades later this friend's mother was having health problems, and my mother was grieving the loss of my dad. My girlfriend arranged for the four of us to take a mother-daughter weekend trip to Canada. We enjoyed a memorable adventure. For my friend and me the best part was watching our mothers giggle like teenagers. It was time to laugh again.

On my fiftieth birthday my adult daughter presented me with a remarkable gift that could not be purchased in any store. I did not want a big party, so she spent months collecting letters from all my friends and relatives, who shared how I had affected their lives. Her gift was love bound in a book.

My dad had been a high school band director for most of his life. I understood his devotion to his students because I was one of them. For his eightieth birthday I networked with other former students to arrange a surprise tribute and band reunion. Alumni, several of whom had become professional musicians, flew in from all over the country to honor the influential role my dad had played in their lives. They shared their fondest memories of my father and, having brought their instruments with them, played as a band again under his leadership. He was deeply touched, and we alumni were happy to renew the bond we once shared in high school. Dad was the catalyst.

During my childhood both my parents were alcoholics. Now I am grown with a family of my own, and my parents are still alcoholics. When my aging mother fell, I brought her home to live with us during her recuperation. I cared for her as a loving parent cares for a hurting child. This experience offered my children the opportunity to become better acquainted with their grandmother, and I received a touch of healing for my own soul.

My sisters and I wanted to honor our parents on their fortieth anniversary and use that occasion to thank them for everything they had done for us. After much deliberation we decided to create a quilt. Each family member contributed a square. Even our husbands and children made squares depicting how our parents had influenced their lives. The youngest granddaughter, nine months old, participated by putting her handprints on a quilt square. That quilt, which now covers a wall in our parents' bedroom, is a tribute to their faithfulness, generosity, and love.

As my wife and I grew older, we found it difficult to accept help from our children. We had always taken care of them. At first we were angry about the role reversal and our decreasing independence, but our adult children were united in their determination to help us and lovingly persisted. One child arranged for the local market to deliver groceries and meals. Another helped with medical visits, while a third helped with financial matters. One thing we did not want to give up was our holiday celebrations, especially Halloween when over two hundred children come to our home and show us their costumes. Every year all our children and grandchildren come to help us prepare for the big day. They arrive in the afternoon to decorate our home and get the fog machine and sound effects ready. We put a big pot of soup on the stove, and everyone takes turns answering the door or escorting our younger grandchildren through the neighborhood. Our grown children make our favorite experiences even more memorable.

When my husband abandoned us, I had to go to work to support my five children. My oldest daughter, who was teaching at a local school, would drive her younger siblings to their school on her way to work. Then she would pick them up at 3:00 P.M. and keep them with her until I returned from work. I could not have survived that season of my life without my daughter's help and support.

Following each special event or trip that I plan for my adult children and their families, I receive a thank-you book from my daughter-in-law. She collects pictures and letters from each family member and creates a book full of memories and sincere words of appreciation for my efforts.

Though she works full-time and has a family of her own, my daughter comes to stay with me one night each week so that my nurse can have the night off. I look forward to our weekly slumber party. My daughter tells me that this time together provides a nice break for her, but I know it is a sacrifice.

My alcoholic father was dying. Though estranged from him for years, my mother (his ex-wife) and we three adult children made the trip across the country to see him one last time and offer love and forgiveness. He warmly greeted us and we discovered that he had become a Christian believer. He died shortly after our visit.

Through caring for my own aging parents and working as a nurse with homebound elderly patients, I have learned that the most important thing I can do for them is *listen*. Their complaints are not demands for me to fix their lives, but pleas for a sympathetic ear and encouragement. Visits from grandchildren are the best medicine. The fresh perspective of youth is rejuvenating. I do not agree with parents who want to shield their children from the "depressing" environment of the sick and dying. The visits distract our aging relatives from their pain, and our children learn to love family members through the natural seasons of life.

Before leaving for college, our daughter created a memoir honoring us as her parents. In a blank book she recorded each character trait she had inherited from us and gave specific examples of how we had passed it on. She thanked us for being wonderful parents and preparing her for life.

It was a family tradition to celebrate the coming of the magi on January 6. In the evening our children would place their shoes by the front door and expect them to be filled with surprises by the wise men journeying to worship the Christ child. That tradition officially brought our Christmas season to a close. The year my husband left us in the fall because of mental problems, we experienced emotional and financial famine as the unthinkable happened. I had to file for separation and secure a protective order against my husband. The holidays were less than ideal, but I tried my best to make them traditional and joyous for my children. What a blessing it was to wake on the morning of January 7 and find that my children had placed my shoes next to their own by the front door and filled them with gifts for the new year!

When my husband and I became older and frail, our children realized that we needed extra supervision. My daughter and son-in-law moved us into a home next door to their own. My daughter checks on us daily and tends to our needs. Our son-in-law maintains the yard and helps with other physically taxing chores. Because of their loving care, my husband and I still enjoy independent lives in the comfort of our own home.

We may give without loving,
but we cannot love without giving.

CHAPTER

10

What to Do When You Don't Know What to Say to . . . Your In-Laws

Be completely humble and gentle; be patient, bearing
with one another in love.
Make every effort to keep the unity of the Spirit
through the bond of peace.

EPHESIANS 4:2, 3

My only son was getting married and I was about to become a mother-in-law. Wanting to start off on the right foot and be my daughter-in-law's friend, I wrote her a letter offering her specific freedoms: *"You don't have*

*to call me Mom unless you want to. You don't have to clean
your house when I come over because then I will feel the need to
clean my house when you visit me. You don't have to spend
every holiday with our family. I know that you have a family
too."* My goal was to welcome her into our family and
clearly communicate that she could love my son and not
worry about pleasing me. I wanted to be an encouragement rather than an obstacle in their new marriage.

Every year my father-in-law gives my wife and me membership to a road service. His practical gift has been a life-
saver when the children have locked keys in my car, the
battery has gone dead in my teenager's car, and my wife
has needed her flat tire changed while I have been away
on business. Dad's practical gift has served as a safety net,
and it's nice to know that Dad still cares about our safety.

My husband is unusually helpful. He doesn't expect me
to wait on him, and he helps with laundry, vacuuming,
or washing dishes whenever he sees a need. This partnership frees me to pursue my own interests and dreams.
I realize from observing other couples that my husband
is a treasure. My sister's husband rarely helps her; he
leaves clothes on the floor and dirty dishes by the bed.
He makes more work for her instead of lightening her

load. One day it dawned on me that my husband had been trained by his mother to respect women and be helpful. She prepared this gift for me. I sent her a bouquet of flowers that afternoon with a card thanking her for the great job she did in raising her son. She was overwhelmed. This experience was also a wake-up call for me to remember that I am training my sons for future daughters-in-law.

My mother-in-law was an avid reader and had looked forward to reading stories to her grandchildren. Since we lived far away from her when our children were young, she recorded herself reading our children's favorite books and regularly mailed these cassettes to them.

Many of our friends did not know how to respond when our infant was born with cerebral palsy. They didn't know how to celebrate the birth of our baby and chose to be uninvolved. My sister-in-law came to our home and asked how to hold and care for our newborn. She offered to baby-sit so my husband and I could have a break. Her commitment to be involved in our child's life expanded our baby's world. This angel became our daughter's favorite auntie and has shared the significant milestones in her challenging life.

My mother-in-law has a critical, negative nature complicated by progressive dementia and agitation. She constantly repeats the same questions and becomes angry when she cannot remember the answers. Visiting her is a way that I can support my husband, especially if he is traveling or immersed in work. Two activities make these challenging visits easier. First, playing her favorite old records calms her, and sometimes she sings the lyrics. Second, although talking about the present is frustrating for her, discussing her childhood and past memories is comforting. She has told me wonderful stories, and I have gained insight into my husband's family history. I used to dread these visits, but now I look forward to learning about my mother-in-law's life.

In anticipation of our wedding, close friends gave my husband's mother a "mother-in-law shower." The theme was that she was adopting a new daughter—*me*. She received coupons to be used when the two of us went out for lunch, coffee, and shopping trips. As we used those coupons during my first year of marriage, my mother-in-law and I spent time together and became fast friends.

Every summer my husband spends one of his allotted vacation weeks traveling with me across the country to my mother's home. Now that my father is deceased, my husband spends the entire week helping my mom with fix-it projects around her house. No job is too small or too big for him. He leaves her prepared for the coming year. She loves him like a son.

As a newlywed our twenty-eight-year-old son discovered that his young wife had numerous physical and emotional problems. Since their marriage she has often been hospitalized for treatment. This experience has taxed our entire family and caused a crisis of faith for our son. He telephones to share his fears, and we pray together. We have promised to be there for him no matter what the future holds. Purchasing a gift for this daughter-in-law is difficult because we have so little in common. I would rather give her money to buy something she wants, but since their funds are limited, any money I give would be used to purchase basic necessities. My son suggested that I take my daughter-in-law out for lunch and a shopping trip. The day was such a success that we have made it an annual event. My daughter-in-law selects something she wants, and our relationship is strengthened.

My mother-in-law was an excellent cook, and I never felt that I measured up to her standards. When she was in the later stages of cancer and after her death, I cooked for my father-in-law. He sat at our dinner table almost every night, and I knew that I was giving them both a gift that was beyond culinary expertise.

After being married for two years, I was still unsure of my role as a wife. I did not know how to respond to my husband's leadership. Confused about submission to my husband, I e-mailed my concerns to my mother-in-law who lives in another state. She sent back a long e-mail filled with gentle encouragement. She assured me that all marriages change and grow as we nurture the relationship through the years. Her wisdom was born of experiences and challenges in her own marriage. She counseled me, "Follow God first. The rest will come." Instead of wrestling with roles and doctrine, I focused on God.

As a pastor I counsel couples before performing their marriage ceremonies. I advise them to develop relationships with their new in-laws by becoming anthropologists. Raised in the city, I married a woman whose parents worked on ranches. My father-in-law was a cowboy. The first thing I did was ask him to help me buy a pair of cowboy boots and a hat that I wore when I visited them. To truly love your husband or wife, you must make the effort to embrace his or her family's culture.

I was expecting our first child when my mother-in-law's friends gave her a "grandmother shower." Each gift was a handcrafted work of art. My mother-in-law made a trip to our home to bring the gifts and help decorate the nursery. One of the gifts was an extraordinary quilt that we hung on the wall. The expectant grandma was as excited as we were about our coming baby.

As a newlywed I was eager to embrace my in-laws with open arms. Their lack of response embittered me through the years. No matter how hard I tried to reach out to them, I felt like a failure. Exhausted from trying to please them, I prayed that God would guide me in loving them. Today our in-law relationship is not what I hoped it would be, but it is peaceful and no longer an issue in our marriage.

When my husband's health deteriorated to the point that caring for him was more than I could manage, my daughter-in-law invited us to live with her family. After adding rooms onto their house, she and our son moved us across the state and into their home. My daughter-in-law was the momentum behind this huge endeavor. She balanced a job, remodeling, and refinancing with caring for her home, her family, and us.

Friendship is the best gift that parents can give their newlywed children. My in-laws and parents made a conscious effort to become well acquainted and soon were fast friends. This working relationship has derailed any competition between families or disagreements about holiday plans. Our children benefit from having two sets of loving grandparents who enjoy spending birthdays, holidays, and vacations together. Because my husband and I are both only children, any in-law problems could have made our lives miserable. Instead our family is doubly blessed. My mother helped care for my mother-in-law after her cancer surgery; my mother-in-law hosted the meal following my dad's memorial service. A new marriage does not intrude on an established family. It expands a caring family.

After his father and brother were killed in an accident, my husband was his grandparents' sole remaining heir. When my husband and I became engaged, his grandmother, a bitter woman, had not yet recovered from her only son's death. I did not know what our engagement would mean to her. The Christmas before our spring wedding she presented us with a hope chest filled with her best linens, silver, and other heirlooms. She had been collecting treasures for months and offered this generous gift as her blessing on our coming marriage.

My own mother was abusive, so my mother-in-law became the caring mother I had never had. She loved me like one of her own daughters. She told me that we were not in-laws, but "in-loves." When my husband and I divorced, I grieved over losing my spouse and my mother-in-law as well.

A reservist in the military, my husband was sent overseas during the war against terrorism. Our income was immediately cut in half because of his absence from work. Our new baby had colic and I was sleep-deprived.

My in-laws noticed my exhaustion and regularly came over to take our active two-year-old for an afternoon at their home or the park. This plan allowed me to sleep while our baby napped. My in-laws fed my toddler his favorite fast-food dinner and often brought me a meal too. Not having to cook (I could barely afford groceries), having adults to talk to, and getting sleep kept me functioning during this bleak time.

When I became engaged, my future mother-in-law told me that she had been praying for me since her son was an infant. Knowing that this woman had prayed for me throughout all the good and hard times in my life, I felt that she was already my second mom.

Though my own dad was distant and critical, my father-in-law became my advocate and friend. He cheered me on as I dreamed of owning a home and starting my own business. We spent many weekends hunting together. When my son was born, he was included in our hunting trips. My father-in-law's fierce belief in me and his faithful support has been the anchor in my life and my example for fathering my own son.

My in-laws annually purchased investment stocks for my children's birthday and Christmas gifts. Those stocks were not expensive, but their value compounded over the years. Just as my children were graduating from high school, my husband died of a sudden heart attack. I assumed that my children's college dreams would need to change. As I evaluated our financial situation, I was relieved to find that the proceeds from those stocks were sufficient to send my children to the colleges of their choice.

As a new bride, being accepted by my mother-in-law was important to me. My husband's mother must have sensed my insecurity because she took me aside on our wedding day and whispered in my ear, "I'm glad to share my last name with you." Those brief words assured me of her acceptance.

After my husband abandoned our family, my sister-in-law phoned long-distance each week to ask how I was doing. She spent hours listening to the latest events in my stressful situation and was the voice of calm logic when I wasn't sure how to negotiate the multitude of confusing decisions in front of me.

Two women in one house—need I say more? My husband's idea of a perfect family included a big country home and his parents living with us. I had to give up my own cozy little world. My mother-in-law had been the model June Cleaver–type mother. I was not. My husband and I led a wild life before we married, and I was not the daughter-in-law his parents would have chosen. As it worked out, my mother-in-law lived her Christian faith by accepting me and appreciating my style of mothering her grandchildren. She was not a bold speaker, but just as courageous as I was, and probably a lot smarter. To help our expanded family function, she folded laundry for me, cooked three nights a week, watched our kids when I needed to run errands, and baby-sat so that my husband and I could have a weekly date night. My husband, who had denied God for years, began to follow Jesus Christ again. Though the beginning was rough, God has abundantly blessed our multigenerational home.

Breakdowns don't happen because of differences.
They happen because family members
can't handle those differences.

DR. BECK

What to Do When You Don't Know What to Say to . . . Your Siblings

Finally, all of you, live in harmony with one another; be sympathetic, love as brothers, be compassionate and humble. Do not repay evil with evil or insult with insult, but with blessing, because to this you were called so that you may inherit a blessing.

1 PETER 3:8, 9

I desperately wanted to go to college but didn't have enough money, and time to register was running out. The only job I could find was baby-sitting in a challenging situation. My sisters and brothers agreed that one of them would always accompany me. We baby-sat in pairs so that I would have a buddy along to share responsibilities. This support helped me fulfill my dream for an education and strengthened our relationships as siblings. Baby-sitting in pairs proved to be so effective for everyone involved that it became the family policy.

My mom always sent me flowers on my birthday and other holidays. After her death my dad continued the tradition. After his death I was surprised and deeply touched to receive a bouquet of flowers on my birthday from my brother. He continues the tradition to this day. We may have had a challenging sibling relationship as children, but now I treasure the fact that he is my family.

When I was diagnosed with a terminal disease, I could not cope with the news, much less console my four children and husband. My sister accompanied me to all my medical appointments. She invited my children, one at a time, to spend weekends with her family. My children took turns expressing grief and frustration to their aunt and uncle and needed a break from the sadness in our home.

While my wife and I were reeling from a serious financial setback, my brother quietly made arrangements to cover Little League fees and the cost of music lessons for my children. Because of his help, they retained a sense of stability in the midst of our struggles. I am thankful that he invested in my children and believed in their future.

When Mother died we, her adult children, felt like orphans. My sister spent four months creating a collage of photos for each of us for that first difficult Christmas without Mom. We shared and laughed, cried and reminisced over memories sparked by those photos. In spite of her own grief, my sister gave us the gift of a strong tie to our past, to our childhood, and to each other.

Our only child has cystic fibrosis. Because of her diagnosis, we decided not to have any more children. However, her best friend has almost become a part of our family. She visits daily, travels on vacation with our family, and stays by our daughter's side when she is hospitalized. This adopted sister cannot take away our child's disease, but she can prevent the loneliness and isolation that often accompanies cystic fibrosis.

When our marriage crumbled, my sister and brother-in-law encouraged us to seek help. With their assistance, we found a two-week intensive counseling program in another state. My sister and brother-in-law kept, entertained, and comforted our children while we attended therapy. A decade later our marriage is strong and our family is intact thanks to these relatives' commitment to our marriage.

The day after my miscarriage, my sister sent me an overnight express package. Inside were a stuffed gorilla big enough to put my arms around and three videos. Her enclosed letter explained that the gorilla was something to hold onto and the videos were for "losing your mind in something other than the pain." There was no big sympathy letter, no I-know-how-you-feel message, no preaching about God's purpose in taking my baby. In contrast one coworker sent a card that stated, "God has a way of getting rid of things that are not right." My sensitive sister's gift was a practical emotional band-aid. I still think about my loss and remember her compassion whenever I hug that giant gorilla.

Suffering from chronic illness, I found myself in the hospital again for a long stay. I knew that my children were safe in my sister's care, but that did not ease my longing for them. Then my sister brought my children to the hospital. They decorated my room with drawings and artwork that they had colored, glued, and glittered. Their festive creations were the best medicine and encouraged me to get well and come home soon.

When my husband went to prison, my brother became my support system. I felt completely abandoned and betrayed, but my brother hugged me and invited me to attend church with him. As a result I dedicated my life to Jesus Christ. My brother also took my children on outings and bought needed clothes for them. He helped me with finances, car repairs, and home maintenance. He visited my husband in prison and wrote letters to him. My brother was my strength when I didn't think that I could go on as the wife of a felon.

When I was recovering from cancer surgery, my sister came to visit me one day a week. Our budget was limited, so she brought nutritious, delicious meals. She purchased a new comforter, sheets, and towels to transform my bedroom and bath. She lovingly pampered me, and her weekly encouragement carried me through that dark time.

Because of my husband's transfer to a job across the country, I left a wonderful part-time job where I had good friends. In the new location I was at home twenty-four hours a day with our two young children. I didn't know a soul in this foreign, cold climate. As my husband became immersed in his new career, I sunk into depression. My older sister never lectured me about needing to get out of the house and meet people, but she did mail encouraging cards with coupons tucked inside. Those coupons forced me to leave the house to buy my children ice cream cones, pick up videos at the movie store, or grab a cup of coffee. Slowly but surely I began meeting other moms on these outings and realized that I could build my life again. My sister provided this incentive without saying one word.

Thirty years ago I vowed to love my wife for better or worse, in sickness and health. My wife now has a debilitating disease that confines her to a wheelchair. She will never again be the woman that I married. Some days her mind is sharp and she is frustrated; on other days her memory is foggy. One week each year, my wife's brother and sister-in-law come to our home to care for her so that I can go on an annual fishing trip with my brothers. This respite gives me the strength I need to return to a difficult situation.

It would have been easy for my half sister to resent me and ignore my children. As a teenager, she remained with her alcoholic mother after my dad and her mother divorced. Later, my dad married my mom and I was born, receiving a golden life while my half sister endured a nightmare. As children our contacts were rare. Now that we are adults, my big sister has built a relationship with me and is an active aunt in the lives of my children. She remembers my youngsters on holidays and their birthdays and invites us to her home when we are visiting in the area. I marvel at her ability to give so generously when she had so much taken away from her as a child. She has taught me that building family relationships independent of past wounds takes effort and can never be taken for granted.

We were more like sisters than friends. We met in kindergarten and from then on my friend was like a part of our family. She knew my life history better than anybody else. On my sixteenth birthday she piled a tower of presents on a dolly and wheeled it down the street to my door. Every gift included a poem and represented a special memory, one for each year we'd known each other. There is no substitute for "adopted" sisters who have known you since childhood.

When my wife's brother became ill with AIDS, he feared condemnation from his conservative Christian family because of his homosexual lifestyle. His sister (my wife) and I brought him to live with us during his course of treatment. Before his death he told us that he had never felt so unconditionally loved by God and his family.

My sister, who is a stickler for maintaining healthy relationships, has been a valuable role model in my life. "I refuse to have a row," she says. "Life's too short to fall out with anyone." Whenever I have an issue with someone (friend or family), her example more than her words encourages me to nurture my relationships. It is worth the work to persevere through conflict and refuse to give up.

God spared our lives, but we lost all our material possessions in a house fire. The fire occurred in the heat of

August and I didn't realize until early December that we had lost the Christmas ornaments that our children had made over a span of twenty years. Those ornaments symbolized memorable events in our lives. Understanding our loss, my sister and friends gave me a Christmas-ornament shower as the holiday season began. Each gift represented a special memory that we had shared. What could have been our saddest Christmas became our most joyous as we experienced the love of family and friends.

Because of my husband's travel schedule, I often found myself alone on such couple holidays as Valentine's Day, New Year's Eve, and our anniversary. I couldn't leave the house because we had young children, so my younger sister and brother-in-law, who did not have children, packed a picnic and came to keep me company on those days. They spread the red-and-white-checked tablecloth on the floor, lit candles, opened a bottle of wine or champagne, and served my favorite foods. Their thoughtfulness never failed to chase away my blues.

My teenage daughter's childhood dream was to ride a horse and join the 4-H horse club. Because of my limited budget and even more limited knowledge of horses, I thought her dream would be impossible to fulfill. Then my friend, who is like a sister to me, allowed my daughter to care for her horse and taught my daughter the basics of riding. When summer came my daughter, decked out in borrowed clothes and straddling a borrowed horse with borrowed tack, rode in the 4-H arena. My friend invested in my child and her dream. Today my daughter owns her own horse and offers other children the opportunity to ride and care for her horse. From my friend she learned to help other young people pursue their dreams.

A month before our baby's due date my husband and I spent the weekend moving into our new home. At my Monday checkup the doctor discovered complications, and my baby had to be delivered immediately. My husband called his sister and my brothers, and when they heard the news, they all jumped into action. While I was giving birth to our daughter, our siblings were unpacking, painting, wallpapering, and setting up our nursery. Our family came from all directions to help us. We returned from the hospital to a welcome-home party with a lavish feast prepared by our siblings.

When my sister was dying of cancer, I moved into her home. Since she could not afford around-the-clock hospice care, I took care of her and her two children. I cleaned her house, weeded her yard, cooked for her family, drove her children to their activities, and put her legal affairs in order. Though I had to put my own life on hold, I will never regret the last months I spent with my sister before her death.

A nasty case of pneumonia caused me to miss giving an important presentation for my college class. The instructor insisted that anyone who was absent had to creatively convince her that his presentation was worth a second chance and a slice of her busy schedule. Still feeling physically ill, this news drained me emotionally, too. My family faced the challenge head-on and began to brainstorm with me until we hatched a plan. I phoned my professor and set up an office visit. My siblings and I arrived at her office ahead of time and positioned our musical instruments. When the instructor arrived, we broke into a toe-tapping tune that immediately arrested her attention. When the last note faded, I launched into my presentation. Thanks to the gifts of time, creativity, and effort from my sisters and brother, I earned a good grade and some extra credit.

Diagnosed with meningitis, my three-year-old daughter had to be hospitalized. Not knowing if my little girl would live or if she would suffer brain damage, I wanted to be at the hospital around-the-clock. My sister stepped in to care for my two older children and kept their lives as normal as possible by transporting them to and from school, baseball practices, and piano lessons. She provided plenty of love during that stressful period. Because of her, I could focus on caring for my ill child without worrying about my other two children.

A job loss caused my wife and me to become homeless. Without judging us, my brother invited us into his home. He made it clear that his help was not a handout—that would have been humiliating for me. I helped him with a construction project on his home and my wife helped care for his children. After numerous interviews I finally found a new job, which would have been almost impossible without my brother's timely help.

A sister [or brother] is a little bit of childhood that can never be lost.

MARION C. GARRETTY

What to Do When You Don't Know What to Say to . . . Your Additional Family

Recalling your tears, I long to see you, so that I may be filled with joy. I have been reminded of your sincere faith, which first lived in your grandmother Lois and in your mother Eunice and, I am persuaded, now lives in you also.

2 TIMOTHY 1:4, 5

When my husband left me, Grandma was my night-light. She listened as I poured out my pain, anger, and bitterness, and never judged my feelings of rage. Grandma's life had been as difficult as mine, yet she was an exceptionally gentle, loving woman. Her example spoke volumes. When I was ready to listen, she wisely suggested how to seek peace and develop a working relationship with my estranged husband. She gave me God's promises, which were lighthouses to guide me. She said everything over my head was under Christ's feet. She reminded me that when a task seems impossible, it qualifies as "Himpossible."

On the first anniversary of our parents' death, my siblings and I spent the day together. We did not want to be alone, yet the more we talked about our parents, the more despair we felt. Then our aunt and uncle telephoned to tell us they were remembering us that day and grieving too. That simple phone call melted away our loneliness.

Grandma and Grandpa hosted "cousins' camp" every summer at their home. All their grandchildren spent the week playing games, enjoying Grandpa's barbecue, and listening to stories read by Grandma. Grandpa began and ended each day with Bible readings and prayer. Our parents enjoyed this time alone to focus on their relationship. The strong bond we developed as young cousins has continued into adulthood. We have a great relationship with our grandparents and a loving extended family. Cousins' camp was such a success that we are continuing the tradition with the next generation.

Against the advice of our family, my wife and I invited my aging grandmother to live with us. Her health was failing and she could no longer live alone. Since I went to work every day, my wife was responsible for the daily care of my grandmother and our three active children. My grandmother was never an easygoing person, and the task was overwhelming at times. Grandma lived with us for three years until her death. My wife was the physical hands of a merciful God.

I was born out of wedlock, and my mom and I lived on welfare. After I graduated from high school, my prospects were limited. Then my uncle offered to pay for my college education. Upon graduation I landed a good job and developed a solid career. My uncle's willingness to invest in my life made all the difference in its direction.

Hospitalized with a serious illness, I was disappointed to miss our family reunion. My niece and nephew videotaped the event with different family members sending personal greetings and get-well wishes. When I viewed that tape a week later, I felt like my extended family was in the hospital room with me.

Grandmother taught me to sew when I was a young girl. Each week I spent one afternoon with her working together on a sewing project. One summer we had sewing camp for an entire week, and added cooking to our schedule. She knew that I was a creative soul and loved making things with my hands; I wasn't as entranced with books as my mom and older sister were. My grandmother said, "I was just like you when I was young." When I became a teenager, my grandmother helped me design and make dresses for special events. With extra fabric I made matching accessories for my date. Whenever I felt stressed by too much schoolwork, I would run to my mom's sewing room and start a new project. My grandmother passed on to me an artistic skill and the gift of understanding.

When our baby had to remain in the neonatal intensive care unit, my aunt gave me a soft teddy bear. "I know it is not the same as holding your baby," she said, "but at night you can hold this with the promise that soon you will bring your baby home." I spent long days in the hospital with my tiny baby and many nights cried myself to sleep holding that teddy bear. When my child finally came home, I put the teddy bear in the corner of his crib. Five years later my son still sleeps with that teddy bear. My aunt gave me the gift of hope.

Annually my grandparents take each of us grandchildren on adventures to places like Yosemite, Disneyland, and Yellowstone or on a cruise. This individual attention is fun because we are completely pampered during the trip, and we are building unique memories that only the three of us share.

My marriage has not been easy. My husband and I have struggled financially through the years. Knowing that my passion is attending the theater, my uncle makes it a point to take me to concerts, ballets, and theater productions, and annually takes me to New York for a week of viewing Broadway shows.

When we were young children, my siblings and I couldn't wait for Christmas. Our anticipation drove our parents to the edge. To help us be more patient, Grandma made each of us a large bag out of festive Christmas fabric and embroidered our names on the front. She collected small gifts throughout the year, wrapped them, and put them in those bags that she delivered to our house on December 13. We opened one present each day for the "twelve days of Christmas," and there was an extra special surprise on Christmas Eve. We opened our gifts each evening during "candle time," when we lit candles, enjoyed dinner, ate chocolate advent calendars for dessert, read Scripture, and prayed for friends and family members as we pulled their Christmas cards out of a basket. Instead of pestering our parents, we celebrated Christmas a little every day.

At a recent church retreat, we were encouraged to write letters to people who had influenced our lives. I wrote to my aunt, who had taught me to play the piano, bought me keepsakes through the years, and taken me on an annual outing. As a child I visited my aunt every week. She was like a second mom to me. After receiving my letter, she told me how much those words meant to her. Many people richly bless our lives, and we need to be deliberate in telling them.

My husband and I could never conceive children. Remaining childless was painful, but even more difficult was entering our golden years without grandchildren. All our friends had growing extended families with children, grandchildren, and great-grandchildren. My husband and I only had each other. Ten years ago my sister's grandson decided that he wanted to adopt a closer grandma because my sister lived in another state. Since I lived in the same community as this young man, he picked me! With my sister's blessing, I relished my adopted role. A child can never have too much love, so I brought him presents, attended his games, concerts, and birthday parties, baby-sat for him, and had sleep-overs for him at my house. God didn't give me biological children, but he certainly overwhelmed me with love in different ways.

I am descended from seven generations of Christian believers. The most influential people in my life of faith were my maternal grandparents. I spent many vacations on their farm where I rose at 4:00 A.M. to pray and read the Scriptures, then sang hymns with my grandpa while we milked the cows. We returned to the house for breakfast, prayer, and Bible reading. My grandparents' faith in Christ was woven into every minute of the day, though their lives were far from perfect. Seven of their nine children died before reaching adulthood and Grandma never fully recovered from the death of their only son when he was eighteen years old. I watched my grandparents pray and read the Bible through their tears. In spite of life's pain they trusted God. In a crisis they were the first people that anyone in the community called. If an alcoholic husband abused his wife, she called my grandparents and they rushed to help. Grandma brought meals to countless families, including the infamous Page Brothers, a rowdy, drinking, swearing, tough group of unlovable guys. She told me, "Now I don't want you to act like the Page Brothers, but they still need to eat." Authentic faith is truly more caught than taught. After my grandparents died, I felt that the baton of faith was handed to me.

When I was expecting our first daughter, my family gave me a "mother-daughter shower." My mom, sister, aunt, grandmother, and friends who surrounded me that day celebrated the mother-daughter bond and discussed its complexity. In a journal, each attendee wrote her advice about nurturing the mother-daughter relationship. I have referred to their comments through the years.

As our extended family has grown and moved around the country, we found it difficult to keep up on all the news about cousins, aunts, uncles, and grandchildren. To keep us connected, my aunt publishes a bimonthly family newsletter. We try to send her important news, but if she does not hear from us, she calls for an update. She compiles the information she has gathered, adds a list of birthdays, anniversaries, and graduations, and mails the newsletter to each family member. In December she assembles the "Year in Review," complete with photos.

Because of pregnancy complications, I apprehensively entered the hospital for a cesarean section. Since it was my second C-section, I understood the risk for my baby and the long recovery from surgery that would follow for me. My cousin convinced my husband to give her access to my hospital bag. She collected funny gifts and cards from my family members and friends and hid the items in different places in my bag. These surprises provided just the encouragement I needed during my recuperation in the hospital.

When I was a struggling college student, my grandparents gave me money for extra expenses twice a year. My grandmother also paid for an oil change and other maintenance needed to keep my car running. Since my parents were paying the hefty private tuition bills, and I was working at a job on campus to earn spending money, my grandparents called their donations little scholarships.

Unable to have children of our own, we "adopted" our nieces and nephews. One niece lived across the country and frequently invited us to visit. When we could no longer make the long trip because of health problems, she brought the trip to us. She sent a book filled with photos of her home, family, town, and surrounding sights. Without getting on a plane, we were able to share her life.

Roses were my grandmother's favorite flowers. On her ninety-eighth birthday I went to see her in the nursing home. The nurses had helped her dress up for the big day. Her mind was sharp, but her frail body was confined to a wheelchair. As we visited, I asked what she longed for most on her birthday. She replied, "I want to go outside and smell the roses one more time." I wheeled her around the neighborhood and we stopped to smell every rosebush we found. Neighbors came out to talk with us, and one kind man cut a bouquet of roses for my grandmother. When we returned to the nursing home, my grandmother told me that this was the best birthday ever. Whenever we talked after that day, she reminded me about our own rose parade.

My mother committed suicide when I was in my late teens. The shock was intensified by the knowledge that I was now an orphan. My aunt and uncle stepped in to fill the empty place in my life. While being careful to continue to parent their own children so that they would not feel slighted, my aunt and uncle frequently set an extra place at the table for me, attended my important events, and gave financial advice. My uncle walked me down the aisle when I was married. Now a widow, my aunt continues to be my family. She flew across the country when my baby was born and over the telephone gives wise counsel to my husband and me when life is overwhelming.

Hospital gowns must be the most uncomfortable and humiliating apparel. I call my cousin "the nightgown lady" because she brought me an attractive, modest nightgown when I was hospitalized. That nightgown made me feel human again.

Our extended family is too large to celebrate each member's individual birthday, so we hold quarterly birthday parties. Every three months our entire family gathers on a Sunday afternoon to honor that season's birthdays. We rotate homes; the host plans the event, provides the main dish, and makes phone calls to assign other parts of the menu. Each family member brings one nice gift and we play a high-spirited white elephant gift exchange game. Then our birthday honorees gather around the cake for pictures and singing. These parties guarantee four family reunions every year. While individual households may struggle with marital strife, illness, children's rebellion, or unemployment, the steady bonds of our extended family have been our foundation. We laugh, we cry, and we support each other through the challenges of life.

I grew up in an abusive home. When as a teenager I finally had a nervous breakdown, my aunt and uncle took me into their home. I was angry and confused, but they patiently helped me to begin the healing process. They encouraged me to seek counseling. Their home was a safe place for me to recover. They loved me when I was unlovable.

An unexpected serious illness and emergency surgery left our family reeling. Since our summer vacation and other activities were put on hold, my grandpa brought us Christmas in July. He donned a Santa hat and carried a bag filled with gifts and treats for each of our five children. He brought balloons and cookies and played games with our kids all afternoon.

I worked hard in high school and was accepted into a prestigious college. No one in my extended family had a college degree, and my parents could not afford to pay the expensive tuition. Yet each of my relatives supported my dream and contributed what they could toward my education. I assumed a loan for the balance. I may have been the fortunate one to attend classes, but my degree belongs to my entire family.

At our annual family reunion Grandma circulates a notebook for everyone to write in. The binder includes photos, poems, and drawings by the younger children. She photocopies the pages and gives each family a set for Christmas. This tradition began five generations ago. The original notebook, containing letters from my great-grandmother, is our family treasure.

I worked as a receptionist for a Christian high school in our town. My niece was scheduled to enter as a freshman and I wanted to do something special without embarrassing her. I asked myself, "What can I do for my niece that no one else can?" While plotting out the new locker assignments in alphabetical order, I broke with policy and gave my niece a locker next to her best friend. On the first day of school in a strange new setting, the girls were thrilled to discover that they were locker neighbors. The treats I left in their lockers were an added delight. The key to caring for family and friends is looking for that unique touch that only you can supply.

Like many other preachers' kids, I went through a period of rebellion as a teenager. I wanted nothing to do with the church. As an adult I learned that my grandmother prayed for me every day of my life, especially when I was wrestling with God. Today I am a seminary professor, and I know that without the diligent prayers of my grandmother, my life would have gone in a very different direction.

My mom gave jars filled with questions about their lives to our older relatives. Answering the questions, they told their life stories, which we recorded in a journal. We honor their lives, and their stories are preserved as a heritage for generations to come.

The day that the police arrested my parents for involvement in drugs, Grandma brought my siblings and me to her home. Over the years she spent endless hours negotiating with the state system to keep us, helping us with our homework, and driving us to school activities and church events. Grandma was our rock of stability in the midst of chaos. I especially remember how Grandma would rock me on her lap while I cried for my parents. She always assured me that she understood my longing and loved me.

My aunt gave me bail money when I was incarcerated. I had thought that she was a little uppity and self-righteous, but she came through for me in my time of need—no questions asked, no strings attached.

Both my husband and I are only children, and our parents were only children as well. This makes for very small gatherings at holiday times, and while our children have the undivided attention of loving grandparents, they do not have aunts, uncles, and cousins. They feel the loss when they observe their friends' large family reunions. We do have several wonderful adopted aunts and uncles—good friends who consciously decided to treat our children as family members by attending their school events and remembering them on holidays and birthdays. I tell our children that these aunts and uncles are extra special because they *chose* to be involved in their lives.

Grandma takes her children and grandchildren on annual trips, during which she plans activities to nurture relationships between the cousins. On one Christmas trip the cousins exchanged names, and Grandma requested that instead of buying traditional gifts, the cousins exchange original poems. (My teenage son wrote a rap on toilet paper.) Though the teenagers initially groaned about Grandma's idea, they enjoyed the family reading of the poems on the last night of their trip together.

To everyone's surprise, when I was a fifty-five-year-old bachelor, I fell in love. When my girlfriend broke off the relationship shortly before Valentine's Day, I was as brokenhearted as a teenager. My nephew and niece sent me a Valentine's Day card that listed the top ten reasons why I was special to them. They understood that I wasn't as tough as I seemed.

Even when my grandmother no longer remembered names and faces, she remembered to pray for each of her children and grandchildren every day. If I had a difficult test at school or I was sick, I knew Grandma prayed for me by name. When she could no longer care for herself, she moved to a nursing home. If she didn't recognize me when I visited her, she would recite her prayer list. When she came to my name, I would shout, "That's me! That's me!" Prayer for her family was the one thing that didn't fade with age.

Elegant dinners are a family tradition. My husband and I were the first couple among the adult siblings to have children. Our firstborn little girl did not disrupt our social outings, but our active twin boys certainly did. Too exhausted to supervise the children at formal functions, I declined most dinner invitations. The pressure of being observed by those who did not yet have children was more than I wanted to face. I felt comfortable, however, going to my aunt's home. When she hosted family events, she had a large tub of toys, videos, and children's snack foods ready to keep our crew occupied. I could relax again and enjoy an adult meal.

As a very young child I went to live with my grandparents. Grandma quit her job so she could educate me. Grandpa, who was my father's stepdad, rearranged his work schedule so he could spend the greatest possible amount of time with me. He took me fishing, hunting, hiking, and exploring. He taught me how to cook and how to remodel a house. My grandma and grandpa taught me about Jesus Christ. They gave me security and stability. They loved me, and I knew it.

My wife and I didn't have children of our own. Every year my niece sent me a Father's Day card. I was flattered to be remembered, and I liked being her second father.

My grandmother and great-aunts were firm believers in the healing power of food. My grandmother brought soup and homemade bread to people facing a crisis. My great-aunt delivered her famous chocolate truffles to family members who were struggling long before we learned about the chemical benefits of chocolate. No matter what our heartache was—a miscarriage or a cancer diagnosis or a lost job or a broken heart—we could count on spoonfuls of comfort accompanied by hugs and listening ears. When my son was stillborn and I could not eat, Grandma said, "Your arms may be empty, but not your stomach." The first day I had one spoonful of soup. One month later I devoured the entire bowl. She seemed to keep track of our emotional state by how much we ate.

No one in our large extended family has time to write individual letters. E-mail is not the answer to keeping in touch because older members of our family, who need the contact the most, do not have computer access. Fixed incomes make long-distance phone calls prohibitive. Since my elderly aunt once said, "Letters are like good visits which never come at inconvenient times," my sister decided that round-robin letters would be the solution. Whenever one of our relatives becomes ill, has surgery, endures a loss, or needs encouragement, she starts a letter around the family around the country. By reading the other entries we catch up on one another's lives before adding our own news and sending it on. Sometimes we paste in photos. Likewise we create round-robin cassettes and videotapes for special occasions. This practice keeps us connected in spite of age and economic differences.

Because of problems with alcoholism and bankruptcy, my parents were unable to finance my college education. They could not even fill out the financial aid applications. When I was accepted into an excellent university, I worked my way through school. My aunt from across the country regularly sent me checks to help with expenses. Being a professional woman, she valued education and wanted me to succeed.

Because her mother died when she was young, my mother never had a birthday party. Yet for my children she hosts birthday dinners at her house and celebrates all the big and small events of their lives. As she did for me when I was a child, she makes annual birthday dresses for my daughters and matching dresses for their dolls. I asked her once how I could repay her for my own wonderful childhood. She replied, "Don't give it back. Pass it on."

God has blessed me with a wonderful grandma. She taught me how God uses one generation to pass the mantle of leadership to another generation. When I

become an ordained pastor, it will largely be because of Grandma's support and her encouragement. We are partners in ministry.

CHRIS MURPHY,
whose grandmother played the piano at parties, restaurants, funerals, and nursing homes to put her grandson through seminary

Expanded Family

And let us consider how we may spur one another on toward love and good deeds. Let us not give up meeting together, as some are in the habit of doing, but let us encourage one another—and all the more as you see the Day approaching.

HEBREWS 10:24, 25

Our church family, and those "adopted" friends who have become closer than family, are precious gifts from God. Along with our families, they are the people God has placed in our immediate sphere of influence as our first avenue of ministry. Church services and activities are mini family reunions every week all year long.

In Romans 16:1–15 Paul acknowledged a number of outstanding believers who endeared themselves to him by acting as family members. One was Phoebe, whose name means "bright." Because she illuminated his weary road by lightening his load, Paul describes her as a "great help to many people, including me." The apostle's Greek word *diakonos*, "helper," is sometimes translated as "servant," "minister," "deacon," or "one who stands by another." Two more examples of church family members are Priscilla and Aquila, who worked alongside Paul. "They risked their lives for me," recorded an appreciative Paul.

Because Phoebe proved herself to be one who faithfully stands by another, Paul entrusted her to carry his letters to the saints in Rome. When we love and minister to our family members, God entrusts us with carrying his good news of forgiveness and salvation to them.

Christians have two families: their natural family and the worldwide spiritual family of God. Our heavenly Father adopts into his family everyone who has been born of the Holy Spirit. There is great joy in standing by the family of God.

In the following pages our contributors offer concrete examples of such support. You will discover unique ways that people have been loved by their church, friends, and family during tough times.

Friends are relatives you make for yourself.

EUSTACHE DECHAMPS

CHAPTER

13

What to Do When You Don't Know What to Say to . . . Your Church Family

Therefore, as God's chosen people, holy and dearly loved, clothe yourselves with compassion, kindness, humility, gentleness and patience. Bear with each other and forgive whatever grievances you may have against one another. Forgive as the Lord forgave you. And over all these virtues put on love, which binds them all together in perfect unity.

COLOSSIANS 3:12–14

One simple gesture made all the difference. I was invited to church events by a variety of friends in high school, but they never offered me a ride. They said, "Come if you can. I'll see you there." As an unbeliever, I was terrified to walk into a church alone. I never had the courage to go. Then one day a friend invited me to a church service and gave me a ride. The next week she invited me to a choir rehearsal and gave me a ride. I became a Christian, joined her church, and have been involved in the music ministry for thirty years.

My husband lost two jobs in one year due to a downturn in the economy. Our own families lived several hundred miles away, but our church family met our every need. Our Sunday school class took up a collection and gave us a large financial gift to pay our ongoing bills. A church committee confidentially paid two other significant debts. Church members faithfully telephoned and prayed for us. My husband's friends set the alarms on their palm pilots to remind them to pray when my husband was beginning a job interview; they followed up with a phone call. One woman from the congregation brought us a huge box filled with ground beef, steak, chicken, and pork, which fed our family during the months of unemployment. A man with a garden called to say that he had a bag of homeless vegetables that needed a good home. Another woman brought us loaves of bread from our favorite bakery. A good friend brought me a "stress basket" filled with lotions, soaps, bath oils, and candles. She acknowledged that I was under as much stress as my husband and needed some pampering. Soon my husband received two good job offers, one in our community and one out of state. Because of our loving church family, we chose to remain in our community. They daily demonstrated 1 John 3:16–18: "This is how we know what love is: Jesus Christ laid down his life for us. And we ought to lay down our lives for our brothers. If anyone has material possessions and sees his brother in need but has no pity on him, how can the love of God be in him? Dear children, let us not love with words or tongue but with actions and in truth."

As a young mother of three toddlers, I lived in a small house that felt like a prison of endless responsibility. Because of my confining duties, I developed relationships with the older women in our extended family, neighborhood, and church who reached out to me. My young friends were on the run with their careers. Those mentor relationships were a surprise gift from God.

When my husband abandoned us, it was weeks before my children or I could tell anyone. We were embarrassed and afraid we would be rejected. Slowly my children each told someone about our situation. I am thankful for those people who said they would pray for us. Our pastor assured us we were part of the church family even in our altered situation. My children remained involved with the Sunday morning worship team. As we had feared, a couple of friends judged me and turned their backs on my children and me. Those who continued to welcome us with the same thoughtfulness we had enjoyed before the separation were the arms of Jesus to my family.

I was an angry, tough, unlovable teenage girl from a chaotic home. Swear words were a natural part of my vocabulary. Then a neighbor took me to her church where I met the youth pastor's wife. Including me in youth group Bible studies and activities, she became a mentor and friend. I'm sure some of the church families thought that I was a bad influence on their children, but the youth pastor's wife continued to pursue me. Today, as a follower of Jesus Christ, I am involved in ministries that reach out to struggling teens.

Whenever missionaries visited our church, our parents invited them to our home for dinner. Through personal contact with these guests, we children were introduced to mission work around the world. When we gave money to help missionaries, we were giving to real people with real faces. Reaching people around the globe for Christ became a reality in our lives.

As a childless widow in my eighties, I live in a nursing facility an hour's drive from my church. Despite the distance, members from my church family continue to regularly visit me. One couple oversees my finances, another friend who is a nurse organizes my medications, one friend shops for my extra needs, and one close friend is recording my life story to encourage other Christians. I have enjoyed our interviews together. Because I never had children, I feared being completely alone in my later years but my adopted children take great care of me.

With a fussy toddler and a strained marriage, we did not find it easy to attend church. Our large family usually sat in a rear pew, one of the few with enough space for us all to sit together. To our shock, we received a letter (not even a phone call) from the deacon board stating that the rear pews were reserved for visitors and requesting that we sit elsewhere. The perfect example of treating guests better than family, it was akin to telling our children not to sit on the couch in case company came over. No one reached out to us in the midst of our marriage/family problems; the board was more concerned with the church seating arrangements.

When my husband was in prison and I did not have enough money to buy Christmas gifts for our children, a family from a local church purchased gifts for our family and welcomed us into their congregation.

I was devastated when I was diagnosed with cancer and my doctor gave me only a year to live. My faithful sister in Christ immediately began to cheer me on through the battle. She came to my hospital room after each chemotherapy treatment. Grinning over a bag overflowing with party favors and balloons, she announced, "One more treatment behind you. We are going to celebrate!" When I was scheduled for radical surgery, she promised to take me on an all-expense-paid trip to an exotic destination when I recovered from the surgery. True to her word, we jetted off to a tropical island for a week of snorkeling at a luxurious hotel. It has been a decade since the doctor predicted I would be dead by the end of the year. My friend gave me the gift of hope. She taught me to celebrate life.

After my husband and I divorced, I was angry with our church family for judging and excluding me. My sons and husband continued to attend that church, but I no longer felt comfortable there. Then I was diagnosed with cancer. The women from the church, without one word of judgment, came to clean my house, brought meals and groceries, and transported me to doctor appointments. They loved me when I was unlovable, and slowly my heart softened. I began attending church again with a new understanding of what a church family is.

While traveling to participate in a parade, three teenagers from our church family were involved in a serious auto accident. Two experienced minor injuries, but one girl fractured five vertebrae in her spine. No one knew if she would walk again. Several of our church family members drove six hours across the state to sit with her parents in the waiting room during her surgery. Someone brought praise songbooks, and we sang and prayed to God throughout the procedure.

As a young person I attended our family's legalistic church. The conservative, exclusively white congregation strictly prohibited smoking and drinking. A loving Christian man came to town and applied for church membership. He was different—a dark-skinned Armenian who smoked cigars. Needless to say, our church community did not welcome him with open arms. Only after much controversy and many church meetings was he finally accepted for membership. This man became my mentor. Whenever he shook my hand, he passed me a quarter. He spent hours praying with me at church, listening to me, and discussing the life of faith. I learned that Jesus Christ has many faces.

During a particularly lean year for us, another family in our church took their December tithe money to the grocery store. When they shopped for themselves, they brought along a second cart for us. They put the same items in each cart. On December 21 they drove their loaded truck to our home and delivered the purchased food. Our kitchen was overflowing and our hearts were even fuller. They fed our bodies and our souls in Jesus' name.

I was living in a dangerous situation. For my own safety and the safety of my children, my church leaders advised me to divorce. To protect me from the usual "she said"–"who said" conversations that can be destructive, my pastor's wife gathered the women in our church so that they could hear my story all together. After asking any questions they had, the ladies affirmed me and each prayed about a different aspect of my life. Finally the ladies asked how they could help and support me. Facing the future was frightening, but my church armed me with a support team.

During the Easter season, in our home we did not give *up* a cherished activity for Lent; we gave an activity *to* somebody. We spent our time mowing lawns for neighbors, taking cookies to a sick friend, writing letters to invalid relatives, and performing other acts of tender loving care. It is not enough to make sacrifices in life unless those sacrifices lead to helping others and sharing the love of God. That is the message of Isaiah 58.

My husband accepted a summer internship in another state, and his decision separated us for months. I was working seventy hours a week in a demanding job to pay our bills, but I didn't know how I could maintain our home without my husband's help. My church family came to the rescue. One couple mowed our lawn and took care of our yard. Two women came regularly to clean our house. One friend had an extra key to my house, and after work I often found home-cooked meals waiting for me in my refrigerator. When my father had a heart attack in a town two hours away, two members from our Sunday school class drove me to visit him. That was the summer I learned about real Christianity, not "sitting in the pew" Christianity. My family in Christ sacrificed their own convenience for me. They literally got their hands dirty. They observed and met needs when I never would have had the courage to ask for help.

I was living in my van and following a rock-and-roll concert tour. Hundreds of miles from home and penniless, I found myself on the side of a highway with a flat tire. I telephoned my dad, who telephoned a pastor he knew in a town near me. The pastor drove out to help me fix the flat and then invited me home for Saturday dinner. I spent the night at the pastor's home. As I was preparing to leave town the following morning, the pastor invited me to attend his Sunday service. After church the pastor and his wife invited me to join them and some of their friends for lunch. Their invitations and hospitality were endless. I never left that town. The pastor helped me find a job, a home in his church, and a saving relationship with Jesus Christ. Because he was willing to take a chance on a hippie living in his van, today I play my guitar in the worship band and teach Bible studies.

Because of health concerns, my family and I already felt overwhelmed when the church informed us that rehearsals for the Christmas program had been moved to a weekday. That meant another trip across town each week for our family, and we were already strained to the breaking point. From that experience we learned to treat family, including church family, as well as we treat guests. We use the best china and furniture for family and friends and make gatherings as convenient as possible for the most stressed person who will be attending.

I have struggled with depression throughout my life. To communicate the fact that she truly understood my pain, a sister in Christ briefly shared with me her own battle with depression. She calls me throughout the week to check on me and often drops off a gift such as a potted plant or a devotional book. She schedules visits so she can listen to me and pray for God to deliver me. No matter what my mood is or how grumpy I am, she stays in close contact.

My husband became a Christian in high school, and I became a believer in college. As newlyweds we began attending a church that we naïvely assumed was representative of all congregations. Older couples in the church, including staff members and their wives, immediately befriended us, invited us to meals in their homes or at restaurants, and encouraged us to use our talents in ministries. This church family truly embraced us. Because of a job change for my husband, we moved to another part of the state and received a very different reception in a local church there. Some of the young couples warmly welcomed us, but the older couples viewed us as a threat. They did not want us to become involved in leading ministries. They did not want change. I have never forgotten the contrast between these two experiences. Now that I am part of the older set in our church, I try to reach out to new families. I understand that God may be requiring my husband and me to step aside from leading ministries that he desires to change.

Exploring Christianity, I began attending a local church's six-week video-and-discussion seminar about Jesus Christ.

Halfway through the course most attendees had dropped out, and I felt silly going alone. Among the leaders was a mature Christian woman who was committed to discipling me whether the church program was available or not. She invited me to come to her home one night a week, borrowed the videos from the church, and helped me complete the course. She listened to me and discussed her faith. This one-on-one mentoring was the key to my conversion. A structured church program can be impersonal, while a caring person who establishes an individual relationship mirrors Jesus Christ.

When my husband and I separated and I was hurt and lonely, my church offered free counseling for my husband, my children, and me. Friends in the church gave me resources that focused on my relationship with God. Through the support of the church, this crisis was the catalyst for spiritual growth.

I was a drug-addicted prostitute without hope. Then a remarkable Christian woman befriended me and invited me, as a recovering addict, to live in her home. When I would become desperate and end up on the streets again, she would come find me. She never gave up on me because she knew that God had not given up on me. Today as a productive member of society, I am working and raising my children—all because Christ reached out to me through this persistent woman.

Our pastor is unusual. He is a "hands-on" minister who puts his words into action. During a Sunday morning rainstorm, he personally came out into the parking lot with a golf umbrella to escort parishioners into the church before the service began. During a grueling choir rehearsal he brought hot cups of cider to the musicians. He is constantly looking for tangible ways to help. Before meeting him, I only knew pastors who were respected scholars, but couldn't be bothered with the petty tasks of life. I have no doubt that Jesus was a "hands-on" shepherd.

The oldest of six children, I grew up in an alcoholic home. The year I graduated from high school my parents divorced, my jealous boyfriend joined the military, and I discovered I was pregnant with his baby. Four babies later, I was divorced, lonely, and feeling like a complete failure. Terrified that I would be judged, but desperate for an anchor in my life, I went to a church. The body of Christians there warmly welcomed my children and me. Together we walked through good and hard times. Two decades later I remain a member of that church. Today I have a vibrant ministry to people outside the church who are hurting because of a troubled past or difficult marriage. The acceptance of a loving church family changed my life.

When my husband abandoned our family and I was suddenly a single parent, the church provided scholarships for my children's schooling, and the men's ministry fixed a plumbing problem in our house. At Christmas the church delivered gifts for the children and gift certificates from local businesses. One woman gave our family a photo album with a note that read, "For your new beginning."

Our courageous church reaches out to real people with real problems. When our marriage was near the breaking point, I learned that our church had a ministry to couples in crisis. Ten couples that had considered divorce but were reconciled made themselves available to help other couples. They left the counseling to professionals, but stood by to love and encourage us. These couples truly understood what we were experiencing, for they had battled serious problems themselves. One man was bisexual, another was an alcoholic who couldn't hold a job, and one woman had had an affair. These couples didn't wear "church masks." Their vulnerability saved our marriage. Our church also has a support group for parents with troubled teenagers; that group is a place where grieving parents can be with others who understand their pain.

During a lengthy hospital stay my husband was not able to attend church. One Sunday night our church praise team came to the hospital to sing hymns, read Scripture, share communion, and lead my husband and our family in worship. We had a mini church service in his hospital room. Other patients and their family members mentioned how encouraging that worship time was for them.

Growing up in an abusive home, I did not know what a healthy family looked like. When I was in high school, my youth pastor and his wife asked me to be their family baby-sitter. Probably suspecting that I had a difficult home life, they often invited me to stay in their home, and I became a part of their family. Through their example they taught me about a godly family.

I had the double blessing of being raised in a Christian family and a committed church family. My parents and their friends modeled what an authentic body of caring Christians looks like. Loving adults nurtured and mentored me in my faith. I learned that their priority was their relationship with God and other Christians. I wasn't simply taught *about* God; I watched His love happen in daily life. Now my husband and I have found a similar church for our family. We adults mentor each other's children and support one another's marriages. Even when our children are reluctant to attend church services or Bible studies, they can't help noticing how the believers in our church family love one another. This is the lesson that will remain with them, just as it remained with me and grounded my developing faith. No matter what happens—whether we have a serious family crisis, a new baby, or some other event—our brothers and sisters in Christ come to share it. Our neighbors once asked, "Who are all those people who keep showing up at your house?" Who keeps showing up? Our family!

The strength of a church isn't seen in the
width of their sanctuary.
It's seen in the width of their arms that circle you.

CHAPTER

14

What to Do When You Don't Know What to Say to . . . Your Struggling Family

But watch yourself, or you also may be tempted.
Carry each other's burdens, and in this way
you will fulfill the law of Christ.

GALATIANS 6:1, 2

My husband and I became friends with another new-lywed couple living in the same apartment complex. Every Friday we had dinner together. Once children arrived, we met for dinner on the first Friday of every month. Fifteen years into our marriage, when my husband and I were thinking of separating, I told these friends we wouldn't be meeting with them any longer because my husband and I were barely speaking. Our friends wanted to continue our monthly dinners, no matter how awkward. They encouraged us to see a professional counselor and promised not to take sides. Continuing the dinners was their way of standing by us. My husband and I made it through that dark tunnel and have now been married twenty-seven years. Our friends didn't give up on us when we had given up on each other. Their faithfulness saw us through that uncertain time.

Mother's Day can be painful for widowed, divorced, or unwed mothers. We are reminded of how very much alone we are when we see fathers everywhere honoring their wives and helping their children celebrate their mothers. My husband abandoned us when my son was three years old and my daughter was six months. My friend, whose husband died in an accident, came up with the idea that we should celebrate Mother's Day with other single mothers. We organized a Mother's Day potluck luncheon, and all the invited ladies brought gifts to trade with one another. Through the years our Mother's Day group has grown. One year we decorated a "Mother's Day tree," under which we placed the gifts. Once we hired a teenage baby-sitter who spent the morning helping our youngest children make cards and simple gifts for us. It is important that our children are not denied the privilege of giving because they do not have fathers.

My grandson came to live with us when his parents could not care for him. Most of our friends did not understand why my wife and I were no longer able to continue our usual social activities such as leisurely dinners out, late-evening card games, and sightseeing trips. They did not understand that we were now busy attending scout meetings, soccer practices, and Sunday school programs. However, one couple easily adapted to our new lifestyle. Instead of vacationing in hotels and going on cruises, we went camping together. Rather than eating at fine restaurants, we barbecued. They embraced our grandson, and our friendship never skipped a beat because it was based on relationship rather than activities.

My husband has many wonderful qualities, but he is not typically romantic. In contrast, my teenage daughter's boyfriend brings her roses every month on the anniversary of the date they became boyfriend and girlfriend. My twenty-fifth wedding anniversary fell in the same week as my daughter's monthly celebration; she received flowers and I didn't. Then a beautiful bouquet arrived from my friend who had been the maid of honor at my wedding. This colorful, cheery anniversary bouquet told me that she had stood by me twenty-five years ago and was still standing by to encourage my marriage.

I didn't anticipate how difficult it would be to have our firstborn child leave for college. A friend told me, "Every time one of my children leaves home, it's like having a limb cut off." She was right. I grieved the loss of my daughter, and I missed all her friends and the vibrant life and chaotic joy that these young people had brought into our home. One of her friends, Chris, stayed in town to attend a local junior college. To my surprise he continued to visit in her absence. He brought flowers to cheer me up on my daughter's birthday because he knew how much I missed her. He was famous for thoughtful acts throughout our community. I recently attended Chris's funeral. At nineteen, he died from cancerous brain tumors. Chris did more in his short life to bring joy to others than most people do in a lifetime of decades.

My husband had been unemployed for several months when he received a good job offer in another state. Since I did *not* want to leave my dream home, our marriage relationship was strained. A friend invited me out for lunch, and over a soothing bowl of soup and a cup of hot tea, she showed me a map of our new town and its surroundings. She had done research on the area, and with a bright marker she had circled places of interest on the map. When I was too heartbroken to think of this move as a new adventure, my friend took the time to focus on the positive. Her creative caring offered me a glimmer of hope.

My mom died when I was a child. After her death my dad seemed to give up on life. We no longer set the table or ate dinner as a family. Sometimes we ate cereal for dinner while watching TV. After my husband left, I was tempted to give up, but I remembered my childhood. I decided that the children and I would continue to eat dinner as a family, set the table with candles, and pray before each meal. I made a conscious effort to keep every one of our family traditions alive. Dissolving a marriage does not mean dissolving a family.

Throughout the challenges of marriage and mother-hood, I had the privilege of participating in a mothers' writers' group. For over ten years we poured out our lives on paper and shared them with one another at our meetings. We met frequently when we lived in neighboring communities, but as job transfers took us to different parts of the country, we met yearly. Our goal was to publish a book of our compiled writings as a gift to our children. The book was to be a living chronicle of our development as wives and mothers. We had shared our joys and sorrows, and now we wanted to inspire the next generation. After a twelve-year process we published our book in honor of Mother's Day. Not only had we comforted each other through the years, but also the process had culminated in passing a legacy on to our children.

The day after my husband moved out, a deliveryman brought a large parcel to my door. A note nestled inside a collection of truffles from my favorite chocolate shop read, "Chocolate hugs during your difficult week." From across the nation, my friend assured me that she cared about me. My children and I were comforted to know that in the midst of the betrayal of a key relationship, our friendship with this precious lady was stable. That evening my children and I shared truffles and tea and counted our blessings, including the love of my friend. Her note remained on our refrigerator for a year as a daily reminder that I was not alone. My friend loved me and was taking the journey with me.

Thyroid problems, in addition to retirement, caused my husband to enter a dark depression. Our golden time of life became a frightening tailspin. I felt helpless. One dear friend, who was disabled and housebound, called my husband every day to check on him, pray for him, and encourage him. Those phone calls were a lifeline for us.

When I made the excruciating decision to have an abortion because I saw no other way out of a painful situation, my family, who were evangelical Christians, ostracized me. Only my cousin came to the hospital with me. Though she didn't agree with my decision, she listened as I cried and grieved about all the losses in my life. Afterward my cousin, who understood that I was recovering physically from surgery as well as recovering emotionally from trauma, came to my apartment daily to bring lunch and check on me.

After struggling for years with an abusive and unfaithful husband, I finally separated from him. As I was unloading groceries one day, my neighbors came over to say they were concerned. I naively thought they were concerned about my children and me, but they said, "A single woman cannot take good care of the yard, and we are concerned about our property values." I was too stunned to reply. Later in the week a friend stopped by to check on my children and me and offered to come every Saturday and spend two hours working on my yard or other home projects. The contrast between these two approaches to crisis deeply affected me.

Accepting the fact that we would not have biological children, we began the difficult and lengthy adoption process. After one adoption fell through at the last minute, we were on pins and needles until the legal adoption of our infant son was finalized. With tremendous relief we celebrated on March 22. Our family celebrates our son's birthday in September, but my friend always brings me flowers on March 22, the day that I became a mom. She understands what a significant day this was in our lives.

On the first Valentine's Day after my marriage ended, my friend sent me a book about the real lover of my soul, Jesus Christ. Her gift reminded me that God did not reject me. Jesus came to bind up the brokenhearted. My friend encouraged me to fill the void in my heart with a strong relationship with the Lord.

My husband is an active individual who never stops moving. My nicknames for him include "Hurricane Man" and "The Locomotive." He has always traveled in both his business and recreational pursuits. We have raised equally active children, who love to accompany their dad on his adventures. Some of their favorite activities are boating and diving. Because I become deathly seasick, I usually stay on dry land. The first time that my entire family left on a five-day trip, I faced the fact that I was completely alone in the house, and this was the first of many lonely weekends to come. My girlfriend, who had recently moved to another city, invited me to spend the day with her. We went out to lunch and took a beautiful walk in the hills outside the city. She put a big band-aid on my heart.

The four of us met when our firstborn daughters entered the same kindergarten class. Though we were struggling to balance our busy lives, we met regularly throughout the year near our birthdays. We supported one another through numerous changes and challenges. Two of us became divorced. Our daughters are in college now, and we still try to meet once a year. The continuity of our friendship has been a great comfort through the many changes in family life.

When my husband became mentally and emotionally ill, the enormous workload of running the home fell on me. I was the one who had to make all the decisions and care for the children. One friend kept pointing me to the Lord. Whenever she came across facts that related to my husband's condition, she passed the information on to me. She reminded me that I did not cause my husband's illness, nor could I cure him. She kept me grounded and kindly shared helpful resources I was unable to find myself.

I gave birth to my son out of wedlock. His father disappeared shortly after I told him that I was pregnant.

Though my own brother remained uninvolved, a friend proclaimed himself my son's honorary uncle. My friend and his wife attended all my son's extracurricular events, invited him to their home for weekend visits, mentored him, and helped him get his first job. Now my son is a young adult applying for college. This couple has been faithful for eighteen years, and my son considers them his family.

I was shocked to discover that my husband was physically abusive to my children. With the support of my pastor, counselor, and friends, I filed legal charges against him and changed the locks on the house. One friend invited my children and me over for dinner that night so I could tell my children in a peaceful place surrounded by caring friends that their daddy would not be living with us anymore. My friend held my children and me while we cried. She and her family prayed with us, followed us home, and made sure everyone was settled in. In the following months this friend helped with household maintenance projects I could not do myself. She made herself available to my children anytime they wanted to call to talk about their feelings. She helped pay for counseling for my children, supported my children's school fund-raisers, and allowed me to telephone her and vent my frustrations anytime I needed to talk.

When I was very ill, she slept on my couch so I would not be alone. She took my children shopping for gifts for me on my birthday and at Christmas. In many ways the Lord has made his presence known in the midst of my difficult circumstances, and he has shown himself through the kindness of people like my friend.

Months before our twenty-fifth wedding anniversary my husband left me for a younger woman. The rejection and betrayal paralyzed me. On my anniversary my sisters and close friends brought flowers and gifts and took me to my favorite restaurant. They couldn't ease my intense pain on that milestone date, but they didn't want me to endure it alone. Unexpectedly, I felt very loved on the anniversary that I had dreaded.

There is a friend who sticks closer than a brother.

PROVERBS 18:24

CHAPTER

15

What to Do When You Don't Know What to Say to . . . Your Grieving Family

Save me, O God,
for the waters have come up to my neck.
I sink in the miry depths,
where there is no foothold.
I have come into the deep waters;
the floods engulf me.
I am worn out calling for help;
my throat is parched.
My eyes fail,
looking for my God.

PSALM 69:1–3

Though my husband died five years ago, my children continue to remember our wedding anniversary. My oldest daughter, who lives in another state, sends flowers to celebrate the day, while my youngest daughter takes me to lunch so that we can talk about her father and my husband. I have told them that it is unnecessary to acknowledge our anniversary, but they insist that our marriage is worth celebrating, as is the man who influenced our lives.

We were mildly surprised when our baby arrived a week early, but the greater shock was that he was stillborn. When my friend heard the news, she immediately grabbed the cash she had in her wallet and sent it along with her teenager, whom she instructed to buy whatever we might need. Being the day before payday at our house, the refrigerator was empty, and we were completely unprepared. It helped to have someone anticipate our practical needs and run errands for us.

When my wife died from cancer, my adult children sent donations to my wife's favorite ministries. I was touched that they recognized her faith and service. Given in her name, these donations are living memorials that enrich the lives of others.

When my husband died unexpectedly, my friend took photos of those who attended the funeral and attached the pictures to letters they wrote to my children and me. On dark days the pictures of dear faces and their soothing written words of support comfort me. My friend also stood by my side as I navigated legal channels and insurance policies. She asked questions that I was too dazed to think of asking and helped me choose the best options for my children.

I knew that my infant daughter would not live to see her first birthday. Her debilitating disease forced us to celebrate every day of her short life. Neighbors and friends joined us for monthly birthday parties. One month I hosted a mother-daughter tea. My daughter died when she was six months old. We made the most of her life and have no regrets.

I always bought a new shirt for my dad on Father's Day. After he died, I felt lost. I grieved on the first Father's Day without him, but on the next Father's Day I went to a men's store and picked out a beautiful shirt. I wrapped it and enclosed a Father's Day card. Then I drove to the veterans' hospital and left it for someone who could use a day brightener.

My mom was a great cook. After her death my sister and I collected Mom's favorite recipes into a book, sprinkled her favorite sayings and Scripture verses throughout the pages, and added family photos. We gave spiral-bound copies to friends and relatives at holiday time. Working on the project was a way to honor our mother, reinforce our bond as siblings, and soothe us during our grief.

My husband has leukemia, and life has been a tough road for seven years. He had been in remission for a while, but when my daughter and I were making college visits, I received a phone call from him saying that the cancer had returned. As we returned home that night, I watched a glorious full moon rise and hang suspended in the sky. Suddenly some huge clouds rolled over the moon. Instead of obliterating its light, the clouds became a backlit piece of art. Just as suddenly the moon appeared from behind the clouds; it was shining as brightly as before. I realized God was showing me that his light and glory are constant, no matter what clouds roll into our lives.

A favorite song was sung at our child's memorial service. Later a friend wrote out the words and framed them in honor of our child. Another friend laminated the obituary and made it into a beautiful bookmark for my Bible. Both of these daily reminders comfort my aching heart.

We five children were busily buying gifts and planning our parents' fiftieth anniversary when my dad suddenly died four months before the party. Reeling from our own grief, we didn't know how to acknowledge this day for our mom. We decided to take her out for an elegant dinner and make the occasion a time when we could share favorite memories, laughter, and tears. Our sensitive waiter brought Mom flowers and expressed his condolences. Months before, I had purchased for my parents a lithograph showing two clasped hands and the following poem:

> *"In this life I will take your hand*
> *As we walk together in the sand,*
> *And when our time on earth is through,*
> *In heaven I will take your hand too."*

I was tempted to return the lithograph, but I decided to give the anniversary gift to my mom. She was comforted to know that my dad is waiting for her on the other side of eternity. She hung the picture in her bedroom where she sees it before she goes to sleep at night and when she awakes in the morning. God chose that bittersweet gift to give my mom hope on a painful day.

Being an only child, my husband was solely responsible for funeral arrangements and estate decisions when his father died. I wanted to help my overwhelmed husband, but not at the expense of our young daughter's care. My sister and brother-in-law invited our daughter to stay in their home so that I could focus on supporting my grieving husband. While we were walking through endless responsibilities, our daughter was not only spared the pain of those heavy days, but she also enjoyed her vacation with an aunt and uncle who loved her.

Knowing that she had terminal cancer, my mom was able to prepare for her death. For each of her five children she left a letter telling us how much she loved us. She also included a different recipe in each letter. She asked us to prepare the recipe on Mother's Day and meet to "celebrate." She didn't want any of us to endure this painful day alone. Arriving at my sister's house, we discovered that I had been instructed to make my brother's favorite cake, my sister had made my favorite salad, and another sister had made Mom's famous chicken and biscuits. Mom was right there among us. We could *taste* her comfort. We make this day of remembrance an annual event.

At my husband's funeral service a friend set out a blank book in which attendees could record special memories of my beloved. After the funeral I placed the book on the coffee table in my home, and friends continued to enter memories of my husband when they visited. This book opened the door to talking about my husband, which was necessary for my own healing. Sometimes well-meaning friends avoided the subject of my deceased husband because they didn't want to bring up a painful subject, but the pain of thinking they didn't remember him was much worse. That simple book offered a natural way to communicate about my grief.

When my baby was stillborn, I learned that a retired delivery nurse had purchased "Children's Corner," an area of the cemetery designated for stillborn babies, who could be buried there without cost to their families.

During her career this nurse had attended many poor families who had left the hospital with empty arms. Because of her compassion and generosity, there is a place for these parents to grieve their loss and sometimes come in contact with other parents who understand the same pain.

Mom left our family specific instructions for her memorial service. We realize now that she did not plan that day to honor her, but to comfort us. She planned a small, intimate gathering at my aunt's home and a walk on the beach. Walking together as we reminisced about Mom's life released our tension and pain. We felt surprisingly refreshed after our unique memorial service. Spared the stress of making arrangements for an elaborate funeral, our family spent the day remembering our mother.

After my miscarriage our children grieved the loss of a new sibling. To ease their grief, we kept an ongoing journal where they could pour out their hurts on paper, and I could write back to them. We held a memorial service for our deceased baby and buried her on our property. My husband conducted the service and read a touching poem that he composed to honor her short life. We planted a flowering tree over her gravesite to remind us that she is blooming in heaven.

My husband died after a long battle with cancer. Ever since, his brother has visited weekly to mow the lawn and help with household projects. Though my life partner is gone, I still feel cared for by his family.

Six months after his death, I was still grieving for my brother. Friends and relatives who had initially rallied to support me had returned to their normal lives and were unaware of my continuing deep sadness. Then I received a letter from my cousin. In it he shared memories of my brother and acknowledged how difficult this loss must be for me. My cousin understood that I lived with a permanent hole in our family.

I had a miscarriage just weeks before Christmas. Instead of joyously anticipating a baby while I was preparing for the holidays, I was immersed in grief. While most friends and relatives were returning baby gifts to stores and avoiding the topic of my miscarriage, a friend made a keepsake ornament for our tree in remembrance of our baby who was already residing in heaven.

Four months before our twenty-first wedding anniversary, my husband died. As a young widow I felt completely alone. A woman from our church brought me a bouquet of red roses on that painful anniversary. I couldn't stop crying as I finally explained to her that my husband had always given me red roses on our anniversary.

My mother was a tremendous cook and expert baker. Until her death from cancer, she was always bringing us cookies, breads, or pies. After her memorial service, my aunt gave me a crystal dessert plate. It seemed an odd gift since I had no plans to entertain guests for a very long time. The enclosed letter explained that on the first Sunday of each month my aunt planned to fill the dessert plate with our favorite cake, pie, or cookies.

On my twenty-first birthday my parents gave me a journal filled with letters they had written on each of my birthdays. My grandparents also had written annual letters celebrating my life and sharing treasured memories. Now that my grandparents and my dad have died, these letters are their voices assuring me that I am loved.

Our mom died when we were young children. Our aunt, Mom's sister, sent a care package every month. She filled the package with favorite foods, some purchased and some baked from the same recipes that Mom had used, as well as holiday treats and toys. I could see the relief on my dad's face when that package arrived. The first week of the month was always a little easier for him.

After my husband died in an accident, his identical twin brother made an extra effort to spend time with our children. My kids know that he is not their dad, but the similarities in their appearance and behavior comfort them. They still have a small piece of their dad. My husband's brother is committed to his role as uncle and mentor.

When my sister was dying with leukemia, my parents understandably did not have much time for me. They practically lived at the hospital. I felt as if I was losing not only my sister, but also my parents. Seeing my grief, close friends and relatives included me in their families. I stayed with them often, and they loved me as they loved their own children.

My dad's sudden death left my mom a young widow with two children. Then my mom married my stepdad, who had never been married before. He had no children and he loved us as if we were his own. He took us to visit my dad's parents every month because he knew that we were their only link to their deceased son. My grandparents grew to love my stepdad too.

I am an adopted child. When my husband and I had a stillborn baby, my adopted parents telephoned long distance to cry with us; and my mom shared with me her own sorrow. She had birthed three stillborn babies prior to adopting me. She told me that she and Dad were sending a check to pay for our baby's burial the same way her parents had paid for her babies' burials. She continued a tender tradition that connected our family for several generations. By sharing her pain, she touched my heart in a deeper way than ever before.

The day after Thanksgiving my brother died suddenly of a heart attack. Needless to say, our family holidays were somber, filled with funeral arrangements instead of tree-trimming parties. That year my cousin gave me a calendar for Christmas. Her attached note said, "Not for celebrating the new year but simply surviving it." On the calendar she had marked one date each month with appointments like "lunch with Lisa" and "go to the movies with Lisa." I knew that I was not facing the year alone.

Christ came out of his tomb and so have they.

MEG WOODSON,
who lost both her children to cystic fibrosis

In Closing

Let us not become weary in doing good, for at the proper time we will reap a harvest if we do not give up. Therefore, as we have opportunity, let us do good to all people, especially to those who belong to the family of believers.

GALATIANS 6:9, 10

You can count on it. As you minister to the family members in your household, as well as to extended family members and those in your church community, you will grow weary. But it is worth the cost. Investing in people, investing in relationships, is the focus of our Lord's ministry.

The common theme that reverberates throughout these pages is that building a relationship requires effort. No matter what challenges are facing you in your intimate relationships, look for opportunities to do good to those involved. *Do not give up.* You will never regret making the effort.

> *Each one should use whatever gift he*
> *has received to serve others,*
> *faithfully administering God's grace*
> *in its various forms.*

1 PETER 4:10

Mary Ann Froehlich, DMA, CCLS, MT-BC, is a board-certified music therapist and a Suzuki music teacher. She is the author of nine books and a series of piano/harp arrangements. She has a doctorate in music and a master's degree in pastoral care. Mary Ann lives in Benicia, California.

PeggySue Wells is a freelance writer and homeschool mother to seven children. She is the author of four books and numerous magazine articles. PeggySue lives in Roanoke, Indiana.